A Message from Dog Trainer Deborah Wood . . .

Our bond with dogs today is so profound that dogs act as the eyes of the blind, are the ears of the deaf, and pull the wheelchairs of those who cannot walk. Every year dogs save people from drowning, awake their human companions in fires, and stay out in the elements to keep lost children warm on freezing nights. Only an ancient bond can be so strong.

It is the Tao of the dog to live with humans, to communicate with us, to share our lives. Each human is given the shamanic ability to communicate with our dogs. We have the honor of sharing the Tao of another living creature.

With that honor comes an extraordinary responsibility. Our dogs deserve to be treated with the same kindness, loyalty, and respect that they give us. Nothing else is morally conceivable.

QUANTITY SALES

Most Dell books are available at special quantity discounts when purchased in bulk by corporations, organizations, or groups. Special imprints, messages, and excerpts can be produced to meet your needs. For more information, write to: Dell Publishing, 1540 Broadway, New York, NY 10036. Attention: Director, Special Markets.

INDIVIDUAL SALES

Are there any Dell books you want but cannot find in your local stores? If so, you can order them directly from us. You can get any Dell book currently in print. For a complete up-to-date listing of our books and information on how to order, write to: Dell Readers Service, Box DR, 1540 Broadway, New York, NY 10036.

The Tao of Bow Wow

Understanding and Training Your Dog the Taoist Way

DEBORAH WOOD

A DELL TRADE PAPERBACK

A DELL TRADE PAPERBACK

Published by
Dell Publishing
a division of
Bantam Doubleday Dell Publishing Group, Inc.
1540 Broadway
New York, New York 10036

Book design by Julie Duquet

Library of Congress Cataloging in Publication Data

Wood, Deborah, 1952–
The tao of bow wow : understanding and training your dog
the taoist way / Deborah Wood.
p.   cm.
Includes bibliographical references (p.   ).
ISBN: 0-440-50841-X
1. Dogs—Training.   2. Dogs—Behavior.   3. Taoism.
4. Human-animal communication.   I. Title.
SF431.W68   1999
636.7′0887—dc21   98-18775
CIP

Printed in the United States of America

Published simultaneously in Canada

January 1999

10 9 8 7 6 5 4 3 2 1

BVG

*This book is dedicated to my teachers
and healers, two-legged and
four-legged, who have helped me
glimpse the bright light of the Tao*

ACKNOWLEDGMENTS

Whoever said writing was a lonely pursuit did not have the kinds of friends and colleagues (human and canine) that I am lucky enough to have. Dr. Charles Wu, a scholar and teacher, inspired this book and taught me a great deal while I wrote it. Three gifted healers—Professor Chen Hui-Xian, Dr. David Eisen, and Dr. Arlette Sieckman—gave me an extraordinary new life and helped me see the world in the way that brought this book to me. Ellie Wyckoff taught me how to train dogs with the respect and dignity they deserve. She also shared many personal experiences to add richness and depth to this book. Roger Lore gave me a great deal of information about Traditional Chinese Medicine and its application to dogs. Leah Atwood, Howard Lucas, and Betty Pakenen looked at this book with fresh eyes and had the kindness to encourage me and the wisdom to show me places where the book could be improved. I had the amazing good fortune to find an agent, Jim Hornfischer, who was enthusiastic from the first day and worked tirelessly to get this book published. He in turn found Diane Bartoli, a terrific editor who has helped me make this book the best it can be. Finally, thanks to my two patient muses, Goldie and Radar, who sat by my side each day as I wrote and demanded that I also spend some time in play.

CONTENTS

One is tempted to use the cliché "from the sublime to the ridiculous" to describe the range of book titles that all begin with yet another cliché, "The Tao of . . ." From *The Tao of Physics* to *The Tao of Pooh*, from *The Tao of Cooking* to *The Tao of Teaching*, from *The Tao of Inner Peace* to *The Tao of Sex* . . . And now *The Tao of Bow Wow: Understanding and Training Your Dog the Taoist Way*.

But I would not use the word *ridiculous* in any pejorative sense to put down any of these "Tao of" books, certainly not this one, although I would bet the ancient Taoist sages would indeed have felt amused if they had lived to see how their philosophy has been applied in the Far West. As for sublimity, if we take the Kantian definition "[T]he sublime is that in comparison with which everything else is small,"[1] then not only does Tao perfectly match the definition, but

---

[1] Immanuel Kant, *Critique of Judgment*, translated by J. H. Bernard, 2d ed., rev. 1931.

many of the books bearing this awesome title also suggest something sublime in that they often imply something mythical, something metaphysical, something a little more profound than their how-to counterparts. The present book is a case in point.

|

The word *Tao* (pronounced and also increasingly spelled as *∂ao*) has often been translated as "the Way" according to one of its meanings. But no matter how you magnify the uppercase *W*, the translation falls far short of the original word in all its denotations and connotations. Briefly one might say that Tao is that which encompasses, permeates, and governs the entire universe. How does Tao do that? Well, that is the Way.

Here we have to invoke a second Chinese phrase—i.e., *wu wei* (this *wei* has nothing to do with the English *way*, although it is pronounced the same). *Wu wei* means "not act" or "do nothing." Tao does nothing to be what it is; it just *is*. As Lao Tzu puts it, "Tao the eternal does nothing, yet nothing is not done." *(37)*

What does that have to do with us human beings? Well, Lao says, "Humans follow the ways of Earth, Earth follows the ways of Heaven, Heaven follows the ways of Tao, and Tao follows its own ways." *(25)* Now if Tao's Way is to "do nothing" but follow its own ways, then we humans should, by inference, follow Tao's example and do likewise—that is, do nothing!

Scholars have cautioned us that the phrase *do nothing* should not be taken literally. Rather it means "not to contrive, to meddle, to make unnatural efforts, to force things to happen when they are not ready." Even so, it would take quite a leap of faith for us twentieth-century beings to refrain from such undesirable action when the ethos of the world we live in tends to tell us to go, go, go! The tendency to force things to happen becomes especially strong when we feel we are in a position of power vis-à-vis other beings, such as our children or "pets" or others whom we think are weaker than ourselves.

The Tao of Bow Wow tells us precisely how to follow Tao's Way in our relations with our fellow beings.

II

The concept of wu wei may contain the following principles:

• Be your natural self. If you want the other guy to be peaceful, cheerful, and loving, all you have to do is be peaceful, cheerful, and loving yourself. It's very simple but not always easy.

• Go with the flow. Things do not always happen the instant you want them to. Bide your time, avoid head-on collisions, seize the right moment, and whatever will happen will happen, with the least effort on your part.

• Break down a big, difficult project into small, easy steps. That's what Lao Tzu means by his famous adage "A thousand-mile journey begins under your feet."

• Let each do his or her bit. In a leadership position, focus on the big picture, and let others take care of the details. That's what Lao calls winning the world through noninterference. *(48)*

In sum, wu wei is a strategy to achieve optimum results through minimum efforts. It is also an attitude that guarantees peace and serenity, quality of life, and quality of relationships.

The Tao of Bow Wow tells us in specific terms how to apply these principles to our relations with our canine companions. But the lessons to be drawn go well beyond the canine. In that sense our dogs can be our great teachers.

III

The "soundless and formless" Tao manifests itself as the more tangible qi (pronounced *chee*). Qi is breath or vital energy. Qi is present both in the human body, which is the microcosm, and in the universe, which is the macrocosm. As Chuang Tzu, the other Taoist sage, puts it, "Human life is the coming together of qi. When qi comes together, there is life; when qi scatters, there is death." *(22)* For life to stay healthy, qi should be ensured free passage throughout the body and free interflow between the human body and the universe. When the flow of qi is blocked, there is sickness.

The exercises developed since ancient times to ensure the free flow of qi are called qigong. Put differently, qigong is an exercise designed to cleanse and unblock the channels through which the vital energy flows. Qigong has as many forms as there are masters who teach them. Whatever their forms, the key to all qigong exercises lies in the same thing: relaxation. Relax the mind, relax the body, relax the breathing, and the flow of qi will take care of itself. This is a typical case of application of the principle of wu wei.

If qi is the stuff human life is made of, it is also that which sustains all other forms of life. Dogs, like humans, are entities of life charged with qi. Just as humans need both rest and exercise to keep their qi in a healthy state of flux, so do dogs. Dogs in general know how to relax and play, often better than we humans do. But they still need training. It is only logical that we should apply the same principle of relaxation to dog training.

The Tao of Bow Wow not only gives expert advice on how to train our dogs after the manner of qigong but offers exactly the kind of philosophical insight we sometimes overlook in our relationship with our animal companions.

IV

As Tao exists in all things, so all things are thus equal. When asked wherein Tao exists, Chuang Tzu rejoins:

> "There's no place it doesn't exist."
>
> "Come, you must be more specific," presses the inquirer.
>
> "It is in the ant."
>
> "As low a thing as that?"
>
> "It is in the panic grass."
>
> "But that's lower still!"
>
> "It is in the tiles and shards."
>
> "How can it be so low?"
>
> "It is in the piss and shit." *(22)*[2]

Surely we don't have to sink that low in the conventional hierarchy of beings to find Tao in our canine friends.

---

[2] *Chuang Tzu: Basic Writings*, translated by Burton Watson (New York: Columbia University Press, 1964, 1996), p. 16.

Chuang Tzu also teaches us the relativity of human values: "Men claim that Mao-ch'iang and Lady Li were beautiful, but if fish saw them they would dive to the bottom of the stream, if birds saw them they would fly away, and if deer saw them they would break into a run. Of these four, which knows how to fix the standard of beauty for the world?" *(2)*[3]

Perhaps this can serve as a reminder that while we look for fun playing with our dogs, we should be sensitive to what is fun for our dogs. Taoist practitioners in ancient China developed all kinds of exercises based on observing and mimicking the movements and postures of animals. Chuang Tzu mentions "bear walking and bird stretching" when he talks about those who exercise for longevity. The most famous set of animal-based exercises in the Chinese tradition is called the Five-Bird Game, designed by the Eastern Han surgeon Hua Tuo (?–208). Similar

[3] Ibid., p. 41.

forms of exercises, such as Soaring Crane, Wild Goose, and Turtle, to name just a few, have been developed in our own time.

Perhaps no one has yet developed a form of qigong that simulates the movements of dogs, but as the author of *The Tao of Bow Wow* has keenly observed, our canine companions' spontaneous movements are indeed reminiscent of what we do in the spontaneous movements of qigong. Not only that, but we human beings have much to learn from our dogs as to how to shed our inhibitions and be our relaxed, playful, natural selves.

Charles Wu, Ph.D.

SECTION ONE

The Tao
of the
Dog

I

TAOISM REDUCED TO MERE WORDS

If you and your dog have reveled in the bright light of a crisp autumn afternoon and shared together the wonder of the moment, you've experienced the Tao. If you've laughed with joy as your dog brought his favorite toy to play with you, you've walked the Tao. If you've held your dog on your lap, gently massaged him, and felt the loving calmness of his presence, you've understood the mystery of the Tao.

Understanding the precepts of Taoism (pronounced *dow-ism*) will make us better friends and trainers for our dogs. Understanding our dogs will help us fathom the endless mysteries of the Tao (pronounced *dow*).

The Tao is a path to be walked, not a word to be defined. To try to define the Tao is to reduce the universe to a handful of ineffectual words.

Lao Tzu, Taoism's most revered sage, wrote more than two thousand years ago:

> The Tao that can be told is not the eternal Tao.
> The name that can be named is not the eternal name.[1]

Still, it is the innate nature of writers to try to explain things in words. Words are the only tools we have. So the following explanation of the Tao is a faint whisper of the beliefs of sages that have come down through the ages.

The Tao is the unifying life force. The more closely we experience and appreciate nature and its life force, the closer we humans are to a state of pure happiness. The more we let the material world, the opinions of others, or our own egos obstruct our sense of the natural energy of the universe, the more unhappy we are.

Taoism is a philosophy that can be compatible

with most religious or spiritual beliefs. Many Taoists are also Christians or Buddhists.

Taoists believe in the equality of all living things. No human is more important than another human. Humans are no more important than our fellow creatures on this planet. Every person and every living thing can become our spiritual teachers.

So when you feel the love of your dog shining through his eyes, your dog is your spiritual teacher. When he takes you away from the worries of your job or your finances, he is showing you the way of the Tao. When he lets you feel the joy of the moment and makes you laugh out loud with the wonder of this world, your dog is sharing with you the wisdom of the Tao.

2

Chinese legend tells us about the Great Separation. Before the Great Separation humans lived in harmony with other animals. We communicated with the other creatures through telepathy and respected all other forms of life as our equals.

Then our egos got in the way. We were forced to live away from the other creatures and forgot how to speak with them. We lost the wholeness we once had. We were separated from the Tao.

Native American legend of the Great Separation is almost identical to Chinese legend—with one important difference. A Native American friend of mine once told it to me this way: "One day the Great Spirit placed Human apart from the animals. The Great Spirit then began to open a huge chasm in the earth to make this separation permanent. Dog looked at Human and then turned back to his animal friends. The chasm grew wider. Dog again looked at Human but again turned back to his animal friends. The chasm grew wider still. Finally, at the last possible moment before the chasm was too wide to jump, Dog took a mighty leap and forever joined with Human. It is that way to this day."

In the Native American version of the Great Separation, we did not entirely lose our connection with nature. We kept a piece of it because of our relationship with our dogs. Our dogs help us understand the extraordinary mystery of the Tao.

Recent Western scientific discoveries indicate that the Native American version of the Great Separation has validity in a literal, scientific sense. Until 1997 scientists believed that dogs had been domesticated for about 14,000 years. Genetic evidence now indicates that dogs have been domesticated far longer, possibly for about

130,000 years. One hundred millennia before early humans domesticated any other animal, dogs were at our side.

As humans populated the globe, we brought our dogs with us. An estimated three-quarters of the world's dog population, including such ancient and geographically diverse dogs as Greyhounds and New Guinea Singing Dogs, trace their ancestry back to a single female wolf who joined an early human at the dawn of our history.

Our earliest ancestors hunted for food with dogs. Dogs joined us when we foraged in the forest and when we settled down in villages and cultivated the soil. When we learned to keep flocks of sheep and goats, dogs protected those flocks from their cousins the wolves and coyotes. Dogs have carried our possessions by carts and sleds. For more than one hundred millennia, dogs have shared the secrets of our souls.

Our bond with dogs today is so profound that dogs act as the eyes of the blind, are the ears of the deaf, and pull the wheelchairs of those who cannot walk. Every year dogs save people from drowning, awake their human companions in fires, and stay out in the elements to keep lost children warm on freezing nights. Only an ancient bond can be so strong.

It is the Tao of the dog to live with humans, to communicate with us, to share our lives. Each human is given the shamanic ability to communicate with our dogs. We have the honor of sharing the Tao of another living creature.

With that honor comes an extraordinary responsibility. Our dogs deserve to be treated with the same kindness, loyalty, and respect that they give to us. Nothing else is morally conceivable.

3

HOW WE HAVE FAILED OUR DOGS

Traditional Western thought has decreed that man has dominion over animals. Animals are not considered equal in importance to humans. The person who has a dog is the "master," and our dogs have been our slaves.

Most dog training in America today is still based on the premise that humans are "masters" of animals. Trainers teach "obedience" through physical domination. One of the best-selling dog books of all time (which is still in print) explains how to hang an unruly dog by a choke collar until it nearly passes out and how to kick the dog "humanely" if it continues to demonstrate problem behaviors.

Electric shock collars continue to be best-sellers, and prong collars that poke steel spikes into dogs' necks are available almost anywhere obedience supplies are sold.

For those of us who love our animals and who consider them part of the family, such "training" is unthinkable. Even without extreme excesses like hanging a dog by a choke collar, it doesn't feel right to jerk a dog around on a chain to make it heel. We certainly wouldn't treat our children or our human friends like this. Why would we do this to our animal friends? Most dog owners I know share the Taoist belief that our dogs are not beneath us and certainly shouldn't receive this kind of abuse.

Over the past twenty years more positive dog-training methods have gradually begun to supplant the dominance-based methods. These methods are far kinder but rely on operant conditioning techniques to train the dog. So dog behavior is "shaped" as if the dog were a laboratory rat.

Most of the trainers who teach dog behavior through operant conditioning methods use a clicker, a little handheld device that makes a clicking noise when the dog performs correctly.

The dog knows, after a time, that the sound of the clicker means he has performed a task well. Instead of hearing a happy voice full of praise, the dog who has successfully completed his task hears a metallic click. This operant conditioning approach isn't based on physical "correction," so it is not as disturbing as training based on dominance, but there is a coldness about it that leaves dog lovers with chills.

I remember sitting around a table in the college coffee shop when a friend of mine came in from psychology class. "You won't believe this!" he exclaimed. "B. F. Skinner confined his child in a Skinner box and taught the child to learn just the same way he taught the rats in his mazes."

All of us were of course horrified by the coldness of a man who would do such a thing to his child. Similarly, it is unsettling for dog lovers to define their relationship with "man's best friend" in the cold language and training techniques of operant conditioning. We want a closer connection than a metallic click.

Operant conditioning reduces the act of training a dog to the dog's superficial responses. It ignores the wonder and mystery of the ancient human-dog bond.

Are there dog trainers who train their dogs with love and respect? Of course there are. However, the language of our culture restricts the ability of these trainers to explain what they are doing. Positive obedience trainers will often refer to the "connection" they have with their dogs or emphasize keeping a good "relationship" intact. Then they go back to the words of operant conditioning because there is no vocabulary among dog trainers for the enormousness of the human-dog Tao.

This book will honor your dog. Using the kind and gentle precepts of Taoism, you can forge a relationship with your dog that will be profound, loving, and joyful.

SECTION TWO

Stillness

4

FORCE IS NOT THE WAY

To those of us who wish to be at peace with ourselves and our animal companions, force is not an option in training. The Taoist tradition has scorned the use of force for more than two thousand years. *The Book of Chuang Tzu,* one of the great ancient works of Taoism, speaks about the use of force in horse training.

Horses have hooves so that their feet can grip on frost and snow, and hair so they can withstand the wind and cold. They eat grass and drink water, they buck and gallop, for this is the innate nature of horses. Even if they had great towers and magnificent halls, they would not be interested in them. However, when Po Lo [a famous trainer of horses] came on the scene, he said, "I know how to train horses." He branded them, cut their hair and their hooves, put halters on their heads, bridled them, hobbled them and shut them up in stables. Out of ten horses at least two or three die. Then he makes them hungry and thirsty, gallops them, races them, parades them, runs them together. He keeps before them the fear of the bit and ropes, behind them the fear of the whip and crop. Now more than half the horses are dead. . . . It is true, nevertheless, that generation after generation has said, "Po Lo is good at controlling horses. . . ."[2]

I have seen dogs trained with force. The dogs I saw usually obeyed their "masters" fairly well. However, all the joy and vitality were trained from the poor animals. Tails didn't wag. Eyes were dull. Movement was joyless. It is a sad and demoralizing sight to see a dog trained by domination, fear, and force.

If we do not start from a point of physical

force and mastery of our animals, where do we start?

We start with mastery of ourselves.

5

FINDING THE STILLNESS

When people think of Taoists, they often picture a person in the pretzellike lotus position, lost in meditation. Meditation and its concomitant physical and mental stillness are basic practices of Taoism. Without the stillness, there is no chance to experience the pulse of the earth and the energy that we all share.

There are many forms of meditation. Certainly the discipline of the lotus position and concentration on the inner core of our being are one important kind. Many Taoists also practice meditative exercises, such as yoga, tai chi, or gigong. In these exercises the body goes through slow movements while the mind is at rest. Taoists call this the stillness within the movement. A walk in the woods or along the ocean can also be a form of meditative exercise. As long as the spirit is calm and the movements are in harmony with the earth, the person who is walking is experiencing the stillness within the movement.

For those of us who love our dogs, a quiet moment with our animal companions is a form of meditation. When we have inner peace and allow ourselves to share that sense of peace with our dogs, we are truly connecting with the Tao.

We cannot help another creature when we are angry. We cannot teach when we are not concentrating. We cannot show by example unless we are behaving in a way that others should emulate. We cannot teach our dogs by shouting, hitting, or jerking on a leash.

When we find the peace and stillness within ourselves, our dogs will begin to sense that stillness. Because of our ancient bond with dogs, they are particularly quick to feel what we are feeling. Our dogs can learn to be calm only when we are calm. Our dogs can learn to relax when we relax. Our dogs can learn to be joyful when we are joyful.

Give yourself the gift of stillness. Then share it with your dog.

6

PRACTICAL APPLICATION OF THE TAO:
Meditative Massage

To share the stillness with your dog, give him a massage. First, be relaxed within yourself. Take some deep breaths that go all the way down to your pelvis. Empty your head of thoughts. Relax your head, neck, shoulders, arms, hands, chest, back, waist, pelvis, legs, ankles, and feet. You'll feel the tension drain from your body.

Then begin to touch your dog. Start at his shoulders, rubbing them gently but firmly. Work down his back, freeing the spinal cord from tension. Remember your dog's tail is part of his spinal cord, so massage to the end of his tail. Massage the sides of your dog's body.

Then go to the dog's head, and rub around his ears and under his throat. Gently massage his ears, starting at the base and going toward the tips.

Massage his tummy and chest. Your dog will let you know where to linger.

Gently rub his legs, paying special attention to the muscles of the thighs of his hind legs. Work your way down to his paws, and gently rub each toe.

As you massage your dog, speak softly to him. Tell him how much you love him. Tell him that you appreciate him. Feel your own inner stillness, and share it with your animal companion.

Just as it is hard for most humans to become accustomed to the stillness of meditation, some dogs take a while to relax during massage. If your dog fidgets, massage in small increments. Just rub his shoulders at first, or his tummy. As he learns to relax with your touch, gradually add parts of his body to the massage. Soon even the most touch-averse dog will learn to relax. He will learn to experience the stillness within your movement.

Massage can help your dog learn to relax in even the most difficult circumstances. My dogs and I had just moved from a condominium in the center of a large city to a quiet coastal town. Radar, my seven-pound animal companion, was tense for the first three weeks in our new home. Then one morning he came up to me and snuggled his head against my arm. It was his way of telling me he needed one of his massages.

For twenty minutes I gently rubbed his little body. He would lean into my hand until it was time for me to move my hand. As I kneaded his tiny muscles, I could feel the tension leaving him. His eyes, which had been constantly flicking about at any noise, became half closed and soft. His tight body became loose. I realized that with each muscle of his that relaxed, the tension eased from the same muscle in my own body. When we were done with his massage, we both were truly comfortable in our new home for the first time. We had found the stillness we were seeking in our new quiet town.

7

LOSING YOUR EGO

As we explore the stillness within ourselves, we find our place within the larger universe. The world does not revolve around us any more than the sun revolves around the earth. The Tao teaches us to love and appreciate others just as we love and appreciate ourselves.

For centuries dog training has been about the trainer. It should be about the dog. There are countless Taoist stories about true masters. In every case the master forgot about himself and concentrated instead on the innate nature of his work. Thus the great boatman knows the water as if he were a fish. The great carver thinks about the wood until he can see the finished carving; then he carves. A great master is always egoless.

Lao Tzu wrote:

One who boasts is not established;
One who shows himself off does not become
    prominent;
One who puts himself on display does not
    brightly shine;
One who brags about himself gets no credit;
One who praises himself does not long
    endure.[3]

Compare this egoless craftsmanship with traditional obedience training. Throughout the twentieth century we have expected dogs to follow our commands like robots. They were supposed to understand us. If we truly want to train our dogs and live in harmony with our animal companions, we must start all over. We must put ourselves in the minds of our animal companions and understand them. That is the most important lesson of all.

8

PRACTICAL APPLICATION OF THE TAO:
The Dog Game

Before we begin serious dog training, we must understand what training is like from a dog's perspective. To understand the difficulty we place on dogs, play the Dog Game.

One person acts as the "trainer," and a second one as the "dog." The "trainer" will think up a task for the "dog" to perform. Do not use a traditional dog-training task (such as sit-stay or

come) since people already know what to expect. Dogs have no clue what task you are trying to teach them. So the "trainer" should have
the person perform a task such as turning in a
counterclockwise circle, walking up to a chair
and sitting on it, stepping over a board, or some
other simple command not generally associated
with dog training.

The "trainer" must not give any information
to the "dog" in the English language. The
"trainer" communicates to the "dog" only by
saying, "Good," when the "dog" is doing a behavior that is associated with the command.
Thus, if the "dog" is supposed to turn in a counterclockwise circle, the "trainer" will say,
"Good," every time the "dog" moves even incre-
mentally toward his left.

When the "dog" has figured out his task, the
person playing the "trainer" will play the part of
the "dog" and the "dog" will become the
"trainer."

What will you learn from playing the Dog

Game? It is very frustrating being a dog, having no real idea what you are supposed to do. It takes only a matter of seconds before most people just want to give up. If the "trainer" uses negative reinforcement, such as giving a loud no when the "dog" is doing behavior that is on the wrong track (not even tugging a choke collar or zapping an electronic collar!), the person playing the "dog" will feel very hostile. You will learn it is easiest to figure out what the "trainer" wants when the atmosphere is happy and the "dog" feels relaxed enough to offer a variety of behaviors. The more negative and hostile the environment, the fewer behaviors the "dog" will offer and the longer it will take to figure out the command.

Playing the Dog Game can be a dramatic revelation for trainers. I was in a training class for people who compete with their dogs at obedience trials. Everyone in the class was an experienced trainer. A woman who was playing the role of the trainer in the game was asked what her reaction was to the person who was playing the dog. She replied, "If my dog behaved like this, I'd figure that the dog was being stubborn and lazy." That woman was then asked to play the role of the dog. She was nearly in tears by the time she figured out her task. She ran over to her dog and gave the animal a hug. "I had no idea what you have to go through," she said to her animal companion.

No one who plays the Dog Game ever views training the same way again. It gives us a great new respect for what we expect our dogs to do. It makes us understand how much harder it is for the dog to learn those tasks when we create an atmosphere of negativity and intimidation.

Successful dog training focuses on the needs of the dog and how to make him understand the exercise in the most direct, enjoyable way. Thus, instead of becoming the dog's "master," the good trainer must try to master the way the dog perceives the world. That is mastery in the Taoist sense of the word.

SECTION THREE

The Innate Nature
of the Dog

9

COUSIN TO THE WOLF

Dogs are not humans dressed up in fur coats. They have their own innate nature. They are happy only when the needs of their innate nature are met.

The Book of Chuang Tzu underlines the importance of understanding the inner nature of the animals we hope to train. "Tigers are a different creature from humans, but you can train them to obey their trainer if you understand how to adapt to them. People who go against the nature of the tiger don't last long."[4]

Fortunately the consequences of not understanding the nature of a domestic dog are not as devastating as misjudging the nature of a tiger. Still, training will be much more successful, enjoyable, and rapid when we train with the understanding of the innate nature of our dogs.

Although our domestic dogs are cousins to

the wolf, dogs are not wolves with floppy ears. A hundred thousand years of separate development have left their mark. Wolves fear new places; dogs love to explore. Even wolves who have been raised in captivity are leery of strangers; most dogs are eager to greet new people. Wolves almost never bark; lots of dogs seem never to stop.

To train our dogs effectively, we must look to the nature of the domestic dog, not the nature of humans or the nature of wolves.

Our Dogs

Domestic dogs have these traits in common:

1. *Dogs are intensely social.* Dogs don't do well when they are left alone for long periods of time. They will do everything they can to be in the company of their packs—whether the packs are comprised of humans or of dogs.

2. *Dogs are hierarchical.* Like the followers of Confucius, dogs go by rank. Even the dog of the most egalitarian Taoist will set up relationships by rank. When ten dogs are together, there is an alpha dog, a number two dog, a number three dog, etc., down to the omega dog. Each animal knows his position in the pack.

3. *Dogs respond to leadership.* If dogs live in a pack, they follow the routine that is established by the alpha dog. Dogs will happily follow a human pack leader. When there is no leadership, the assertive dogs will make their bids for leadership, using force if necessary. The submissive dogs in the pack will become more apprehensive until leadership issues are resolved.

4. *Dogs are intelligent and need something to occupy their minds.* Dogs have the intellectual capacity to execute a pack hunt, in which they stalk prey and may even drive the prey into the waiting jaws of hidden pack mem-

bers. They have the ability to keep track of vast herds of sheep and move the sheep over hundreds of miles. Even if your dog's body has been bred down to a small or nonutilitarian form, she still has the formidable intelligence of her working cousins. If dogs aren't given traditional jobs, such as sheepherding, livestock protection, and hunting, they must have creative ways to use their intelligence.

5. *Dogs like variety.* They like to explore new places and meet new people and new dogs. Dogs who don't have the opportunity to get beyond the confines of their yards often become very aggressive or very fearful.

6. *Dogs have prey drive and need to have the opportunity to chase.*

7. *Dogs need exercise.* Some dogs, like Border Collies, are built to run twenty miles a day. If a dog who is built to get a lot of exercise is kept confined, he will become frustrated and neurotic. Even small dogs need exercise every day, although they may be able

to do their running in a living room or a small yard.

8. *Dogs need to play.* One of the most noticeable differences between dogs and wolves is the amount of time dogs spend in play throughout their lifetimes. There are few versions of dog solitaire. Because dogs are intensely social creatures, they need a human or another dog (or both) to share their games.

If our dogs get adequate attention, kind leadership, creative opportunities to use their brains, lots of exercise, and plenty of play, they will be happy and content. They will be living according to their innate natures. It is the responsibility of the humans in the household to provide the dog with activities that meet these needs.

10

THE NATURE OF OUR WORLD

Many people fear that training will hurt the innate nature of their dogs. They believe they are limiting the freedom of their dogs by teaching them training exercises. That might be true if we were living in the wild and our dogs were taking care of us.

Creatures in the wild do not need training. Wolves, African Wild Dogs, or even domestic dogs that have successfully reverted to the wild do not need humans telling them what to do.

But our dogs haven't chosen to live in the wild. They've chosen to be in our homes.

The human world is fraught with peril. Our dogs need protection from speeding cars. If a dog uses his natural prey drive to hunt the neighbor's livestock, he will probably find himself staring up the barrel of a rifle. A dog who acts on his instinct to protect himself when a small child invades his space will face the fate of a "vicious" dog. Your animal companion's life may truly depend on gentle, loving training.

Even when training is not a life-and-death issue, it is important to the well-being of your animal companion. The human world is a noisy, scary place. Dogs need some assistance translating incomprehensible human actions into a perspective dogs can understand. Without training, your dog must constantly deal with his fight-or-flight response. Your dog has to decide if each person who comes across his path is a threat to you, your family, or himself. Each noise has to be evaluated for its threat. Each new place you go has to be searched for danger.

Unless you can communicate to your dog that he is safe and can relax, he will be on alert twenty-four hours a day. Just like the driven Type A human who never can relax, this overload of the fight-or-flight response is devastating to your dog's mental and physical well-being. Just like their human counterparts, dogs develop neurotic behavior patterns and stress-induced illnesses when they are stretched beyond their emotional limit. That is the fate of the untrained dog in the human world.

In addition, your dog should be trained because it will make him happier. Dogs are pack creatures, and it is their innate nature to work together with other members of their packs. Doing simple training exercises with a human—walking on a leash, coming when called, doing a sit-stay—all replicate the relationship of pack dogs on the hunt. Your dog will bond with you, trust in you, and have a happier relationship with you if he has the opportunity to learn to work with you.

11

PRACTICAL APPLICATION OF THE TAO:
Becoming a Taoist Alpha

Hidden inside a flat-faced Pekingese or a long-eared Basset Hound is a wolf's view of its pack. It is one aspect of our dogs' wolf heritage that remains intact.

Packs are hierarchical places. There are no equals in a wolf pack. Each animal is ranked from alpha to omega. Each member of the pack knows and respects the role that every other member has.

It is normal for a healthy young wolf to do his best to become the alpha wolf in the pack. At about one year of age a young wolf will begin to elbow his way up the pack hierarchy. His challenges will go into full gear at about age two, when he becomes physically mature.

Your dog will do the same thing.

The odds are that at about a year old, your

loving, sweet puppy will begin sizing you up to take your job as leader of the pack. At about age two or three he'll begin to try to take over in earnest. Depending on the breed of your dog and his individual personality, he may even get dangerously aggressive. Dogs in this stage of development may sometimes be unsafe near young children because the dogs realize it is easy to dominate a child physically.

It is essential to your animal companion's physical and mental well-being that he does not become the pack leader. Even though you are a gentle, nonhierarchical, Taoist type of person, you must be the leader. Help your dog find his respected role in the hierarchy of your household "pack" in a position other than the alpha role. One of the cruelest, most destructive acts that a well-meaning human can do is to allow his animal companion to take over the household.

Look at the responsibilities of being pack leader from the dog's perspective. Your dog views his household in the identical way a wolf

views his pack. In a wolf pack the leader initi-
ates hunts for food. He is in charge of keeping
the area physically secure from other predators
who might compete with the pack. He decides
which pack members may come and go from the
territory. He has the responsibility for the wel-
fare of the pack. He also has to fend off the
efforts of other wolves in the pack who aspire to
take his position as alpha. In the wild the job of
pack leadership is one that an intelligent wolf
can handle with success.

However, no dog can successfully lead a human household. The humans in the household
need to come and go to work and school and to
perform other daily tasks. A dog trying to control these comings and goings will be frustrated
and anxious all the time. He may try to nip or
may even bite family members or strangers to
enforce his decisions about who should be allowed to come and go and when they should be
allowed to do so.

In the wolf pack it is the alpha who has the

right to the pack's food, and he allows the other pack members access to the food when he chooses to. In a human household this translates into a dog who "steals" food from the table (he's not stealing it from his point of view; it's already his) and who may bite someone who tries to take away his food or toy (the alpha cannot allow such behavior from a subordinate). When the dog is reprimanded by his humans, the alpha dog is confused and may feel he is supposed to put the upstart humans in their place before they can take over his position as alpha leader.

Not all dogs try to become alpha. About 15 to 20 percent of all dogs are born with an innate tendency toward introversion and shyness. When given no leadership, these dogs are forced to take on the alpha position. The submissive dog does not want to take over. He wants the protection of a pack leader who will make decisions and protect him from the world. Being forced into the alpha position only adds to this dog's anxiety. Extreme fearful behavior, such as constant submissive urination, fear-biting, and dread of strangers and new places, are all created or exacerbated by humans' inadvertently putting a submissive dog in the pack's alpha position. People who don't provide leadership for their shy or submissive dogs increase their dogs' fear levels exponentially.

Dogs are sentient beings. Whether your dog is naturally seeking the alpha role or is a submissive dog who has taken it by default when there was no human leadership, he knows he is not being an effective leader. A dog who has been allowed to assume the alpha role in a human household is very anxious. Often this anxiety shows up in stress-related health problems and behavior problems. Tens of thousands of dogs are euthanized every year because they exhibit uncontrolled alpha behaviors. Countless others have had their lives cut short because of ulcers, autoimmune disease, epilepsy, and other illnesses that are caused by or exacerbated by stress.

So a kind person must become the pack alpha without using force.

Taking the Leadership Position

The *Tao Te Ching* tells us that mighty rulers cause others to follow them without using force or without dishonoring them. Lao Tzu wrote:

> The Tao is constantly nameless.
> Were marquises and kings able to maintain
>   it,
> The ten thousand things would transform on
>   their own.
> Having transformed, were their desires to
>   become active,
> I would subdue them with nameless
>   simplicity.
> Having subdued them with nameless
>   simplicity,
> I would not disgrace them.
> By not being disgraced, they will be
>   tranquil.

And Heaven and Earth will of themselves
   be correct and right.[5]

So what is so namelessly simple that a dog will
react to it? It is using cues that tell him that you
are automatically entitled to the alpha role. In
the wolf pack the alpha member controls who
gets food, when pack members may come and
go, and who gets attention. You must do the
same thing.

The alpha dog eats first, so be sure to feed
your dog after you eat, not before. This is not
cruel (your dog will get his dinner); it just gives
information to your dog so he understands that
you are the alpha. If you have been leaving food
out for your dog to eat at will, change this practice. Your dog should realize that you control
the food because that is what leaders do.

Secondly, have your dog perform a task before you feed him (whether it is dinner or just a
little treat) or before you give him affection. You
are not being a bully. In the dog's eyes, leaders

give directions. (If you do not believe this happens in the wild, just watch a nature television show when African Wild Dogs are on a hunt. Each dog clearly has a defined task to perform. Somebody is giving directions.) When your dog performs the task (such as sit), give him the reward. He will be happy; he has a job to do and is rewarded for it. It will reinforce to your dog that he has an important role in your pack and that you are a leader he can rely upon.

Do not let your dog leave and enter rooms ahead of you. The top dog goes first, and that should be you. Make the dog wait behind you and then follow you.

This gentle approach is nonconfrontational. You don't provoke a big showdown or pit your physical strength against the dog's. In the words of Lao Tzu, you don't "disgrace" your dog. Therefore, he is less likely to rebel against your assertion of dominance than if you force the issue.

I have seen anxious, nervous, and aggressive

dogs make extraordinary changes in their behavior just from following these procedures.
One of those dogs was Jake, an eighty-pound
Chow Chow–Labrador Retriever mix. Irene
brought Jake for training lessons when the dog
was two years old. Jake, with his powerful body
and strong neck, could pull Irene anywhere he
wanted to. At our first session Jake would not
establish any eye contact with Irene; he was not
about to give her an opportunity to become his
alpha. I learned that Jake could not be trusted
near children or small dogs. Irene diligently followed the gentle alpha techniques. Jake had to
work for his food and for privileges. She taught
him training exercises using rewards and praise.
After three months Jake was a changed dog.
For his final lesson we took him to a very busy
pet superstore. There were at least a dozen other
dogs at the store that evening. Some people,
with puppies bouncing at the end of leashes,
came over to pet Jake. One small child, with no
parent in sight, ran up to Jake and threw his

arms around Jake's neck. Through all the fuss and distractions, Jake kept his eyes firmly glued on to Irene's face. He patiently endured whatever she asked of him.

Jake no longer had to be tough and aggressive twenty-four hours a day. He could relax because Irene had taken over leadership responsibilities for their household.

When you become a leader your dog can trust and depend upon, your dog can relax.

SECTION FOUR

Qi

12

THE KEY TO COMMUNICATION

All of us who love our dogs recognize the special energy that makes our animal companions different from any other creatures on earth. Your dog may exude sweetness, or intelligence, or vigor, or mischievousness. The energy that defines the soul of your friend is his qi.

Qi (pronounced *chee*) is the energy that makes up the essence of each thing. We exude qi from our body, and we absorb the qi of other things. This exchange of qi is the basis of all relationships.

The exchange of qi is essential to our well-being. Just as we benefit from the oxygen a tree emits as waste, and the tree benefits from our carbon dioxide, the exchange of our essences helps animals and plants flourish.

When we listen to a great speaker who holds us spellbound, we are exchanging qi. He gives out his qi to us and energizes us, and in turn we return our qi to him and energize him.

When your lover walks in the room, you can feel his presence before you see him. When someone is staring at you, you can feel a prickling sensation on the back of your neck. You are exchanging qi.

Although the exchange of qi is the exchange of pure energy, we usually show physical signs of the interaction. When we see a dear friend, the smile of recognition and the happy hug are tangible signs of the energy exchange between us. When you come home from work and your dog greets you, his doggy "smile," wagging tail, and wiggling body all are visible signs of the qi that is passing between the two of you.

Dogs and humans have developed stylized forms of communication to enhance the exchange of qi. Yes, we feel pure energy from each other. But both species also vocalize, give body language, use touch, and send telepathy to strengthen the flow of qi.

Our dogs are constantly trying to exchange qi with us. They watch our every move; they wag their tails and wiggle their bodies; they send out telepathic signals to us. Watch your dog when you begin to respond to his signals. He will be so pleased that his human is finally learning to communicate.

We can make our dogs much happier and we can become much more effective dog trainers when we use both the tangible and intangible methods of exchanging qi.

Tangible Exchanges of Qi

Vocalizations. Dogs and people have a wide variety of vocalizations. Dogs have warning barks, greeting barks, play barks, whines, growls, and odd noises known only to their human companions. People whisper, yell, scream, cry, and laugh. All these vocalizations mean something within our own species.

Take the time to listen to your dog's vocalizations. He gives you all kinds of information if you only listen for it. Dogs bark differently when a dog is in the yard from when a human is. Your dog has warning growls and play growls. Your dog hears and smells things that are far beyond the ability of any human to detect. Learn your animal companion's language so you can benefit from what he has to tell you.

Dogs also learn our language, and they do it far better than we learn theirs. You do not believe dogs are really understanding language? A trained dog performs specific actions when his human companion quietly speaks a word or phrase. A well-trained dog may respond to more than sixty different words or signals. Some dogs respond to more than two hundred.

But dogs cannot understand our language if we do not teach it to them. If we are to have a pure exchange of information with our dogs, if our words are going to enhance our exchange of qi instead of get in the way, we humans need to be clear. The same word must always have the same meaning. *Sit* must always mean "sit." *Come* must always mean "come." *Stay* must always mean "stay."

Keep your voice light and happy, but strong and clear. Your dog will shut down his qi if he thinks that the exchange of his energy with you will be unpleasant or frightening.

With happy tones and consistent use of words, your dog will learn the meaning of the words you teach him. Your verbal communication will expand the flow of qi between the two of you.

Body Language

Dogs have much more expressive body language than humans. We might be able to catch up if we only had tails!

Because dogs give one another so much information with their bodies, they look to our body language to understand what we are trying to communicate. We can strengthen our exchange of qi with our dogs by using our bodies as a conscious form of communication.

First, smile. It does not take a puppy long to figure out that a smiling human is a happy human. Dogs, being intensely social creatures, definitely want to be a part of whatever a smiling human is doing. Somehow smiling also seems to brighten the flow of energy between dog and human.

Move quickly. Walking slowly and moving lethargically decrease the flow of energy. Brisk, happy movements increase the flow of energy.

Touch your dog. Pats, scratches, ear rubs, and hugs all help relay energy between the two of you. One of the reasons we love dogs so much is that they are tactile beings. They share their energy with us through touch. Return the favor to your dog with lots of touching.

At the same time you are giving information to your dog through your body language, he is giving you information with his. Watch for what your dog is telling you.

Ears. A happy, confident dog holds his ears forward. A frightened dog lays his ears back.

Lips. Every human understands the meaning of a snarl. Often overlooked is the opposite: a doggy smile. With lips slightly parted and the tongue showing, a smiling dog is a happy dog. A facial cue that is usually misunderstood is a yawn. A short, quick yawn is a sign of nervousness and anxiety, not of weariness and boredom.

Tails. A wagging tail is a sign of excitement; that excitement may be happiness or aggression. A tail tucked between your dog's legs is a sign of submission and fear. He is interested in an object if the tail is horizontal with his back. A tail held up high with the fur bristled out is a sign of imminent attack.

Posture. One of the world's joyful sights is a dog in a play bow: front legs glued to the ground, back legs straight, tail up and wagging. One of the frightening postures to behold is a dog about to attack: teeth bared, hackles up on his neck, body tensed to spring. A submissive dog will show his subservience to other dogs and humans very clearly by lying on his back, putting his tail between his legs, and avoiding eye contact.

Respect what your animal companion is telling you through his body language. He will trust you more if you are responding to the information he is giving you.

When you are with your dog, see if he is enjoying himself. Is his tail up and happy? Are his muscles relaxed? Is he smiling? The exchange of qi works best when both parties are happy and relaxed. Watch for what your dog is telling you.

Eye Contact

Dogs exchange qi and communicate through eye contact. Just remember the last time you were eating a sandwich and your well-fed dog gave you his most pathetic stare, making it clear he was probably going to starve to death if he did not get a bite of your sandwich immediately. That stare is communication—and exchange of qi—at its finest.

Although both dogs and humans communicate through eye contact, the use of eye contact among dogs is a little different from among humans. A stare directly into the eye of your dog is extremely dominant behavior in dog terms. I have seen people say to their dogs, "Now look at me when I say that!" and force the dog to gaze directly into their eyes. To a dog this kind of eye contact is excruciatingly painful. He will feel he is being punished and will have no idea why you are punishing him.

On the other hand, a very dominant dog may view the same direct eye contact as a challenge. Some dog-training books suggest staring down a dominant dog. That is fine—unless the dog decides to meet your challenge and respond with an attack.

While direct, strong eye contact is not appropriate, soft, loving eye contact is. Dogs exchange qi through loving eye contact all the time. Soften your expression. Look at your dog briefly, look away, and then look back at him. Gentle eye contact will enhance the power of your words and the exchange of the energy between the two of you.

Prey Drive

When wild canids work together, they are hunting. The act of cooperation is inextricably linked in your dog's mind with his prey drive. You can use his prey drive to increase his relationship to you and to increase the energy (the qi) of your work together.

Holding bits of delicious (to a dog) food or favorite toys in your hand for your dog to focus on is not a gimmick. It is helping him associate your hands with the magic of the chase. For example, if you give him a little treat each time he touches your hand, soon he will always reach up and touch your hand whether or not there is food in it. Of course your dog will know when there is a treat in your hand and when there is not. Dogs have not survived one hundred millennia without being able to figure out where the food is. He will touch your hand because it represents the qi of the hunt and the delight of sharing prey.

The more you show your dog how you want things done, using the combined power of a food lure, the excitement of favorite toys, and the magic of your hands, the easier it will be for him to work with you.

Hand signals should be part of the information you give to your dog. Although a dog can learn to associate a hand signal for any exercise you have taught him, he will understand hand signals most easily if they are associated with the movements you make when you train him to do the exercise. For example, I train my dogs to lie down by luring them to the ground with a tidbit. Soon, when I move my hand to the ground, the dogs will lie down. Similarly, I train my dogs to sit by holding a food lure above their noses; their hand signal for sit is a raised hand. Once a dog knows a verbal signal for any training exercise, he can easily learn a hand signal for the same exercise. When my dogs know how to come at the word *come,* I add an arm movement when I call them. Soon they will come to the specified arm movement alone.

Because dogs respond so strongly to body postures, giving your dog both a hand signal and a verbal signal will double the information that he receives from you. If your dog is deaf, he can be trained to respond to hand signals alone.

13

PRACTICAL APPLICATION OF THE TAO:
Clarity of Meaning

It is hard enough to be a dog trying to learn human language. She should not have to deal with having the meaning of the words of that language change all the time. Use language to enhance the exchange of qi, not to interfere with it.

Each word you speak to your dog should have only one meaning. For example, many people use the word *down* to mean "to lie down." They may also use the word *down* to tell the dog to stop jumping up on guests. Using one word to mean two different things is very confusing to your dog. Soon she will believe that your words have no meaning.

Therefore, if you teach the dog to lie down using the word *down*, don't use the word *down* to indicate the dog is not allowed to jump on company. Use another word instead, such as *off*. Otherwise the word *down* loses all meaning to the dog.

How can your dog believe that you are an intelligent being whose words have meaning if you keep changing the definitions all the time? If you want your dog to believe your words have power and are part of your qi, you must always be consistent with your words.

One of the basic rules of exchanging qi with your dog through the use of words is to *respect your dog's name.*

The typical human companion says, "Spot!" and the dog is supposed to know that means "to come." Then the person may say, "Spot!" and it means "What a good dog!" A few minutes later "Spot!" may mean "Get off the sofa!" The next time "Spot!" may mean "Stop chewing my new shoes!" and later "Spot!" means "Time for dinner!"

No wonder so few dogs respond to their names or to anything else their humans say. Our vocalizations have been so random that they are meaningless.

In order for our words to increase the exchange of qi between us and our dogs, each word we say must have a specific significance. Our dog's name should be used only to get her attention, just as we know to look in a friend's direction when she calls out our name.

To help your dog learn that her name has special and positive meaning reserved just for her, say her name, and give her a little treat when she looks at you. Repeat this several times a day for a few days, and your dog will always give you her undivided attention when you speak her name. After those first few days you don't need to give her treats when you say her name. Just smile when she looks at you and tell her how special she is. Of course it is fine to spice it up with a little treat every now and then.

Be careful of nicknames for your dogs. If you sometimes call your dog Spot, and sometimes call her Freckle Face, and still other times call her Speckle Toes, she may have difficulty figuring out that she has a name that belongs just to her.

Be consistent. Treat your animal companion's name with respect. Do not assign it ever-changing, random meanings, and your exchange of qi and level of communication with your dog will multiply.

14

TELEPATHY:
The Pure Exchange of Qi

Shamans have the power to communicate telepathically with animals. Because of the unique and ancient bond that we share with our dogs, all of us can have the shamanic ability to use telepathy both to send and to receive information.

Dogs Receive Our Thoughts

Dogs communicate by telepathy. They give and receive information through this pure form of communication and energy exchange.

For all the skeptics who need scientific proof, studies in England have shown the power of telepathy between dogs and their humans. People went to various sites where they were assigned directions at random. Sometimes the directions

would instruct a person to go to another loca-
tion. Other times the directions told the person
to go home. Within thirty seconds of their human companions' receiving the instructions to
go home, most of the dogs in the study woke up
from naps or stopped their other activities and
went to the door to wait for their humans to
return.

Dogs communicate with one another telepathically all the time. Think of wild dogs or
wolves in an elaborate pack hunt, where a couple of the dogs chase the prey to the dogs hiding
downwind in the brush. There are no exchanges
of barks. No one has a map of the game pre-
serve, with little markers for the battle plan.
Clearly the dogs are communicating telepathically.

If you have more than one dog, you can see
this telepathic exchange going on all the time.
When your dogs split up and each takes one side
of an intruding dog or cat (whether in play or

something more serious), they are dividing up the task through telepathy. If you are tuned in to your dog, you can feel the exchange of energy.

Dogs get telepathic signals from us all day, every day, and they act on them. We can make training easier for them by forming a mental picture of what we want them to do. When you want the dog to sit, ask him to sit and think of him doing a beautiful sit. The odds are he will respond with the gorgeous sit you were hoping for.

Telepathy can be very important when the dog is moving. He wants to know where you want his body to be in relationship to yours, just as when he is hunting in a pack. If you visualize the dog in heel position or coming to you from a distance and sitting at your feet, he can get a better idea of what you want him to do.

You can choose to be a skeptic and not give your dog mental pictures of what you want him to do. But why not try it? You have nothing to lose by offering him a mental picture of what you are asking of him. You have the possibility of gaining a better exchange of qi and strengthening your relationship with your dog. There is certainly enough scientific proof of the ability of dogs to receive our telepathic signals that it seems foolish not to try to give this extra tool to your dog.

Dogs Give Us Information Through Telepathy

Many people find it easier to believe that dogs can receive our thoughts than to believe that we can receive our dogs' thoughts. Of course children know that animals communicate by telepathy. Young children do not find it odd that all the animals in their books talk. It is in the process of growing up, in which our world loses its magic and mystery, that we lose our ability to hear our dogs. It is a wonderful opportunity to use the Taoist shamanic tradition to choose to listen to your dog.

To feel the telepathic communication with

your dog, put yourself in the Taoist state of still-ness. Sit still. Breathe deeply, feeling your breath down in your pelvis. Allow your brain to relax and think of nothing. Then relax your neck, shoulders, arms, hands, chest, back, waist, pelvis, legs, ankles, and feet.

Feel the rhythm of your dog's breathing, and sense the electricity of his mind. Be open to what he has to tell you. Soon, when your dog looks at you, you will know when he wants to go for a walk, when he's sick, when he's feeling anxiety. When you play games like fetch to-gether, you can think of where you will throw the ball and your dog will head to where your mind is thinking. As you share each other's rhythms, you will learn your dog's sense of hu-mor. Dogs do laugh, and we can learn to laugh with them.

Whether you try to establish a telepathic rela-tionship or rely on the more obvious exchanges of qi, your relationship with your dog depends on the quality of your communication.

15

Blocking the Flow of Qi

The exchange of qi is the essence of our communication with our dogs. Therefore, if we want to have a wonderful relationship with our animal companions and to communicate clearly with them, it is important that we do not block the flow of qi. Any action that pulls our dogs' energy away from us disturbs the flow of qi between us.

The following are ways that many dog trainers lose the exchange of qi with their dogs:

1. *Violence.* Any act of violence causes a dog to pull back into the shell of her body. Obviously there can be no free flow of qi when there is fear.

2. *Yelling and Overexcitement.* Qi flows from our inner stillness to the inner stillness of another. When we lose our inner stillness through anger, tension, or even nervous ex-

citement, we lose our ability to exchange qi with our animal companions.

Although we must avoid overexcitement, we should be animated with our dogs. As long as you are keeping your focus on the dog, you can certainly jump and run and play. When you are playing with your dog but maintaining the flow of qi, you are experiencing the meditative state of action (communication with your dog) within the stillness (your inner calm) within the action (your happy movements with your dog). The key is to keep your communication channels open with your dog. If you are too excited, angry, or nervous to focus on your dog, then you are not exchanging qi.

3. *Too Little Response.* Your dog has to know that you are receiving her communication. If she does not think you are noticing her efforts, she will stop trying. Tell her how proud you are when she has done a good job.

Pet her; laugh with her; talk with her. Let her know you are there for her.

4. *Gimmicks.* Beware of dog-training gimmicks. The most popular at the moment are clickers that operant conditioning trainers click when the dog has done well. Another popular gimmick is a wand the operant conditioner uses as a target for the dog's attention. These devices, well-meaning as they may be, focus the dog's attention on the gimmick instead of on the trainer. This diminishes the flow of qi between the trainer and the dog.

Interestingly, clickers were first used in dolphin training. Dolphins of course use clicking sounds in their vocalizations. Use of clickers with dolphins may be a good idea since the clickers sound a lot like a dolphin's speech. It is sort of like trying to learn a foreign language before you visit another country: You may not be an expert at communicating with the people of that country, but they will appreciate the fact that you tried. At least the trainers were trying to communicate a little bit like a dolphin. Because clickers worked well in training dolphins in a nonviolent manner, operant conditioning dog trainers adopted it part and parcel.

Using clickers with dogs is like learning the Japanese language to go visit China. It just isn't the same. Rather than use gimmicks, use your voice, body, eyes, and telepathy to communicate directly with your dog. You don't need a clicker to talk for you.

The exchange of qi is the sharing of pure love. It is the process of communication. It is the joy of being united in the Tao with your dog. It is one of the greatest gifts we share with our dogs. It is a rare and sacred treasure to share the qi of another animal. We must do all we can to honor this gift our dogs give to us.

SECTION FIVE

Wu Wei: Powerful Nonaction

16

THE PRINCIPLE OF WU WEI

One of the basic tenets of Taoism is that the least action is usually the best action. To illustrate this concept, think of the power it would take to move a two-ton boulder. It would take massive equipment and huge effort, and still, it might be impossible to move the boulder. Then envision a small stream flowing around the boulder. The stream quietly skirts the edges of the boulder and still gets to where it wants to go. Eventually the stream will erode the boulder, and the mighty rock will yield to the tiny stream. This is the principle of wu wei (pronounced woo way), often called the action of inaction.

Lao Tzu wrote in the *Tao Te Ching:*

Under heaven nothing is more soft and
yielding than water.

Yet for attacking the solid and strong,

   nothing is better;

It has no equal.

The weak can overcome the strong;

The supple can overcome the stiff.[6]

The closest concept we have in the West to wu wei is the maxim "Work smarter, not harder" (which I find to be much more irritating advice than "Be as the flowing stream").

Western, dominance-based dog training is exactly the opposite of wu wei. Think of the way dominance-based trainers teach a dog to sit. The trainer pulls up on the dog's choke collar and shouts, "Sit!" When the dog does nothing (because the poor creature has no idea what *sit* means), the trainer pulls again on the collar and pushes down severely on the dog's rear. "I said sit!" the trainer yells. The dog might sit then, but it can be a long and constant struggle before the dog regularly sits when he is asked to. This is a particularly difficult process with dogs who are dominant or large, the hardest dogs to control physically.

Now imagine a no-force lesson to sit. The trainer is calm and connected with the dog. He holds a small treat or toy in front of the dog's nose, pulling the treat back over the dog's head so the dog naturally sits, and gently says, "Sit."

The principle of wu wei makes dog training much easier for the human, less traumatic for the dog, and the dog learns faster. Why would anyone use any other means of training? As soon as we put aside mastery of the dog and think about mastery of the art of training, all training becomes much simpler.

Applying the following concepts will help you train in accordance with the principle of wu wei:

1. *Figure out what would motivate the dog to do the action without force.* Use his interest in food, his prey drive, his desire to be petted, or his sense of fun to teach him each exercise. Remember to concentrate on the innate nature

of the dog, not on your own desire for dominance.

2. *Use your exchange of qi to help the dog.* Be happy and active. Give him gentle eye contact. Touch him. Give him clear, consistent words to connect with each action. Hold a telepathic image of what you want him to do.

Keep your dog's qi flowing. This means short, happy work sessions. It means lots of play breaks. It means talking to your dog. Smile and relax with each other as you learn new things together.

3. *Teach the dog in small increments.* Children don't learn to read Shakespeare in a day. First they learn the alphabet. Next they learn small words. Then they learn small sentences. It takes a lot of work and practice reading before a child can read Shakespeare.

The same is true for your dog's learning. Add little increments of time or difficulty. For example, well-trained dogs can do a down-

stay in a line of a dozen strange dogs while
their owners are out of the building. No dog
can learn to do that in a short period of time.
It takes many steps and a lot of practice. First
the dog must learn to do a down. Then he
learns a stay for five seconds with his owner
right in front of him. That stay is now
stretched out to ten seconds, fifteen seconds,
etc. Next the owner gradually does the stay
while two feet in front of the dog, then four
feet, six feet, ten feet, twenty feet, etc. At each
addition of time and space, the dog is given
time to adjust to the change.

It may seem slow to teach a dog in such
small increments. Remember the flowing
stream, however. With these tiny increments
of learning, soon the dog is trained in the
most difficult tasks without force and without
distress. While people who push their dogs
too fast or try to teach through intimidation
are having difficulties at the final stages of
training, the person who utilizes the princi-

ples of wu wei gradually passes them, with a dog that is happy and confident.

4. *Deal with a problem before it is a problem.* Lao Tzu wrote:

> Deal with it before it happens.
> Set things in order before there is
> confusion.

> A tree as great as a man's embrace
> springs from a small shoot;
> A terrace nine stories high begins with a
> pile of earth;
> A journey of a thousand miles starts
> under one's feet.[7]

It is very difficult to stop a dog's action in the midst of the action. Trying to control a dog when he is in full attack on another dog is almost impossible. Trying to grab a dog as he leaps into flight after a rabbit is beyond the physical ability of most mortals. All you can do at the point when your dog is out of control is try to manage the situation—and resolve to deal with the issue before it is a problem the next time.

If you know you have a dog who may act aggressively toward other dogs, get his attention before the other dog walks into the room. If you have a puppy, don't let him mouth at your hands or jump up on you now. It is much easier to deal with a ten-pound puppy than a hundred-pound adult. Think about what will happen next, and deal with the problem while it is still of manageable proportions.

17

PRACTICAL APPLICATION OF THE TAO:
Teaching the Meanings of Words Using No Action

Dogs learn the meanings of words very quickly. When your dog is sitting still, go up to her and say, "Good sit! What a good sit!" Pet her while you praise her (as long as she stays in position). When she is standing still, say, "Good stand! What a good stand!" Again, pet and praise her while she is in position. When your dog comes up to you to greet you, say "Good come!" and pet her lavishly.

Although some dogs learn more quickly from this technique than others, most dogs can learn the meanings of the words for many of the basic training exercises just by hearing them whenever they are naturally doing the behavior.

One of the best ways to stop a problem barker is to teach whisper using this technique.

All dogs have to open their mouths and inhale before they bark. When your dog opens her mouth and begins to breathe, say, "Good whisper!" She will look at you in surprise but will almost never bark because she got the attention the bark was designed to give her. If you do this every time you see her begin to bark, within a week or two, your dog will whisper (open her mouth and inhale) rather than bark. I've taught two problem barkers to whisper using this technique.

One of those problem dogs was Wilson. We lived in a downtown condominium. Although Wilson was a small dog, he had a big bark. He used that big bark to call out to dogs who were being walked along the sidewalk below. He used it to announce the daily arrival of the garbage truck. He used it to suggest I should play with him. It sometimes felt as though he used that big bark of his all day, every day. I was concerned that I would receive complaints from my neighbors. Then a friend told me about training a dog to whisper. Every time Wilson opened his mouth to bark, I told him, "Good whisper." Wilson was a very clever dog, and within two days he whispered at all the things he used to bark at. When I said, "Whisper," he would wag his tail and make his silent bark. Wilson still knew the difference between a real bark and a whisper. Whenever a stranger came down our hallway, Wilson would let out a real bark. That was just fine with me.

SECTION SIX

Teaching Basic Exercises Using the Principles of Taoism

18

Words That Can Save Your Dog's Life

Throughout the world there are six basic exercises that are recognized as essential to a dog's safety: sit, down, stay, heel, come, and stand. These are words your dog must understand and respond to.

A dog who is sitting and staying cannot engage in a fight. A dog who will drop down flat in the middle of a run can be stopped by his human companion before he runs into traffic. Heeling quietly at his human companion's side allows the dog to go places without incident. A dog who will come reliably every time he is called can be extricated from trouble and given more freedom than a dog who will not come reliably. A dog who will stand still and allow a veterinarian to assess injuries is likely to have a long and healthy life.

You owe it to your dog to help him understand these lifesaving words. Using the Taoist principles already described in this book—stillness, working with the innate nature of the dog, using the exchange of qi, and applying wu wei—you can quickly and joyfully teach your dog these lifesaving words.

Before your dog learns these words, however, he must learn the art of paying attention.

19

PRACTICAL APPLICATION OF THE TAO:
Teaching Attention

Just like people, dogs can do only one thing at a time. A dog who is looking lovingly into her human's face is exchanging qi with her human and cannot focus on another dog, a cat she might like to chase, or anything else that can get her in trouble or put her in danger.

It is very easy to train your dog to give you

full attention. Hold a bit of smelly, soft, dog-friendly food in front of your eyes. (Remember, you are training from the dog's perspective and are giving her a treat she likes, not necessarily a treat a human would like.) While the dog is looking at the treat in front of your eyes, say, "Watch me." The dog will certainly do so. Give a little of the treat to the dog. Do this several times a day for a few days. Soon every time you say, "Watch me," your animal companion will give her full attention to your face. After a few days alternate holding food in front of your face with just putting a finger by your face. *Always* give the dog a big hug, and tell her that she is a wonderful creature whether or not she is re-warded with food, and say, "Good watch me!" every time she looks at your face.

If you are consistent with the training and generous with the reward, your dog will put her full attention on your face and lovingly exchange qi with you every time you say, "Watch me."

When you go on walks and a dog is coming

down the street, say, "Watch me," and your dog will not challenge the other dog (she cannot develop the eye contact for a challenge because her eye contact is with you).

If your dog tends to jump up on company, say, "Watch me." Your dog cannot jump up on company when she is staring at your face, lovingly exchanging qi.

Most of the worst dog behaviors can be brought under control by simply teaching your dog to look at your face.

Application of Taoist Principles in Teaching the Words *Watch Me*

Stillness: In order for your dog to watch your face, you must be calm. If you seem angry, your dog will avoid your eye contact. If you seem overly excited, your dog will look around to see what has you so excited. Connect your inner stillness with the inner stillness of your dog when you say, "Watch me."

The Innate Nature of the Dog: Your dog's prey drive will cause her to look at your face since you will be holding food there. Soon your dog will associate the words *watch me* with your leadership and the relationship she wants to have with her gentle alpha leader.

Exchange of Qi: The food represents the adventure of hunting in a pack. Soon your words will convey that same excitement and energy. Your gentle eye contact and loving praise will make your dog feel joyful as she looks in your face and concentrates all her qi on you.

Wu Wei: It is much easier to control a dog who chooses to look adoringly at your face than it is to pull a dog by a collar.

Now you have your dog's attention, you can far more easily teach her the lifesaving words of *sit, stay, down, heel, come,* and *stand.*

PRACTICAL APPLICATION OF THE TAO:
Teaching Sit

Most dogs can learn to sit in just a few minutes. First say, "Watch me," so your dog is looking at you and giving you his full attention.

Hold a favorite morsel of food in front of the dog's nose and draw it back over his head. Gently say, "Good sit!" as the dog's rear end naturally goes to the ground as he reaches for the food. Ninety percent of all dogs will naturally sit as long as a human holds the morsel of food just an inch or so from the dog's nose and arcs the food directly backward over the dog's head.

Repeat several times a day (using a food lure each time until the dog truly understands the word) until your animal companion sits instantly and happily as soon as you say, "Sit."

Occasionally a dog will get a little confused at first. Remember when you played the Dog

Game (page 26) and how confusing it was to try to figure out what your "trainer" wanted from you. Sometimes a dog will turn and spin rather than sit. If he spins, be sure you are holding the morsel of food just above his nose and directing it straight back from the dog's nose. If the dog is still confused, try practicing the word in a place where he cannot turn around. You can also try *gently* helping him into position by pushing forward on the back of his thighs.

Do not force the dog into position. The old-fashioned way of pushing down on a dog's rear end can contribute to spinal and hip problems. The dog will also think that sit is a form of punishment. (Wouldn't you think you were being punished if someone pushed you into a position despite your struggles to be free and made you stay there?) *Sit* is an important, happy word with meaning. It is not a punishment.

Do not worry about stay at first. Just watch for an enthusiastic sit, and reward your wonderful friend.

As a dog tries to learn a new exercise, many people are tempted to say "no" far too quickly and stridently. When your dog is trying to learn a new exercise, he doesn't know what action is bringing about your "no" response. When you were a child struggling to learn math, you would not have wanted your teacher to bark "no" to you when you honestly tried your best but got the wrong answer. Some verbal communication with your animal companion as he struggles to figure out what he is supposed to do might help him. So if he spins instead of sits, tell him, "Oops, that's not quite it," and start again with luring him into position. There should be no negative pressure placed on a dog while he is learning an exercise.

It is fair to tell your animal companion "no" once he clearly knows what he is supposed to do and then chooses to do something else. If he knows a training exercise completely and thoroughly and does not perform his job, it is fair to tell him "no" and perhaps briefly tug at his collar. Now show him what he is supposed to do, and praise him when he does the exercise correctly. This gives your dog the information that he is really supposed to do the exercise every time you ask and that when he does it, his gentle alpha leader is pleased and proud. *However, until your dog thoroughly understands what you are asking of him, using negative pressure only reduces the flow of qi between you and makes it harder for him to learn his new exercise.*

Application of Taoist Principles in Teaching the Word *Sit*

Stillness: As in all training, it is essential for the human to feel inner stillness before he can connect with the dog.

The Innate Nature of the Dog: This exercise relies on the dog's prey drive. He is reaching up to catch the food, putting himself into the sit position.

Exchange of Qi: The trainer's fingers will soon represent the food to the dog. After a few days most dogs will go into a sit position by following the trainer's fingers. This hand signal is the dog following the qi of the trainer's hand.

Wu Wei: Nothing is easier or gentler than teaching a dog to sit using this method. It is much faster and physically far less demanding on the trainer than dominance-based methods of training.

21

PRACTICAL APPLICATION OF THE TAO:
Teaching Stay

When your animal companion can sit and stay in one place for a couple of minutes at a time, life is much easier and safer for both the dog and her human. Once your dog understands the meaning of the word *stay,* you have much more freedom to take her places and introduce her to new things. You will know that you can keep her in one place no matter what dangers may develop around you. *Stay* is the word that is most likely to save your dog's life if a dangerous situation occurs.

When a dog learns to stay, she develops patience and self-control. She overcomes her fight-or-flight response and learns to trust you to guide her through this difficult human world. Using the principles of Taoism, most dogs can learn to stay very reliably but still retain the joyful flow of qi between themselves and their human companions.

When your dog is doing a stay, she should remain in place without making any major motion. The more motion she makes in training, the more likely it is that she will leave the place she is supposed to be staying in altogether when a new situation presents itself. So try to help your dog keep in place consistently during practice.

Be careful to respect the use of the word *stay*. Many people say, "Stay in the car, Spot." Then they leave, and Spot is free to jump all around the car and terrorize anyone who comes near the vehicle. Obviously Spot is not doing a stay. Other times people will say, "Stay." The dog may stay still for a couple of seconds, and then she walks away, sniffs the grass, and visits someone interesting. The dog's human companion of course is ignoring all this behavior from the dog.

A dog cannot learn the meaning of the word stay *(or any other word) if his human companion does not use the word consistently.* It is not at all fair to the dog to complain about his progress in learning to sit and stay, if sometimes *stay* really means "Hold still for just a second," and sometimes it means "Wait in the car, I'll be right back," and sometimes it means nothing, because the human said the word but didn't help the dog stop jumping and wriggling.

If you find yourself using the word *stay* in many situations, use a different word when you want the dog to stay in one place without moving. Use the words *wait* or *place* or *stillness*. What word you select does not matter. It does matter very much that you use it consistently.

To teach your dog to stay, first have her sit. Stand in front of your dog with her treat out of sight. *Calmly* say, "Good sit. Good stay. Good sit and stay." Before she gets up, pull a treat out of your pocket and give her lots of love and praise. The first sit-stay should last no more than about five seconds.

If she was successful the first time for five seconds, make the second sit-stay last for ten seconds. Give the dog a little treat at five seconds, but tell her, "Sit, stay," as you give the treat. Give her another treat at the end of the next five seconds; then release her. Over time build up the number of seconds between treats and the overall length of time the dog is doing a sit-stay.

Of course your dog will probably be unsure of what you want at first and may try to stand up or move to you. Try to catch her movement before she stands up. (Remember Lao Tzu's advice to "Deal with it before it happens.") So when your dog begins to shift her weight to get up, say "Sit," and (if she truly understands the word *sit*) she will settle back into the sit position. Then reinforce her with a "good sit, good stay."

If she actually stands up, say, "Oops, that wasn't what I had in mind," and gently return her to the sit position. She is still trying to figure out what *stay* means, so do not give her any negative pressure, or she will learn to run away when you say, "Stay." If she stands up when you say, "Stay," you can lure her back into the sit, but don't give her a treat for going into the sit position (otherwise your dog will think that *stay* means "sit still for a moment, then stand up and get a treat for sitting again"). If the dog is up and jumping around, start all over with a sit, and then give her shorter intervals on the stay, not giving her the chance to make a wrong choice.

One of the biggest mistakes that most traditional dog trainers make is to reward the dog for her hard work only at the end of the sit-stay. So the dog has to sit, not fidget, and wait patiently, none of which is rewarded. Usually the trainer will say, "Stay" in a threatening, upsetting tone. Finally, when it is all over, the dog is released from the sit-stay and only then given love and treats. What does the dog learn from that? She learns the word *stay* is boring and involves no fun and no treats. When she hears the word *stay*, she will droop and withdraw her qi. Reward the dog for staying while she is staying. Say, "Good stay," and give her a treat. Repeat the word *stay*, and leave her again. Then go back and reward the stay. When stay becomes something fun to do, which may be rewarded at any moment by a proud human companion, stay becomes an enjoyable, qi-filled exercise.

Over time gradually increase the distance and length of time the dog does his sit-stay. Start out always performing this exercise on leash. Later drop the leash on the ground when you leave the dog. Finally, when you are sure the dog understands and enjoys the exercise, you can do a sit-stay while the dog is off leash several feet away from you.

Application of Taoist Principles in Teaching the Word *Stay*

Stillness: Stillness is especially important in stay, since the dog has to feel comfortable staying a distance away from her human. Be still and calm, or else your dog cannot resist moving.

The Innate Nature of the Dog: This exercise relies on your dog looking up to you as her gentle alpha leader. She is using her hierarchical pack behavior to understand she must stay in place, even though you are away from her.

Exchange of Qi: Telepathy is very important in this exercise. Your dog needs your reassurance that it is all right to be separated from you. Visualizing a sit-stay will help make this clear. It is also extremely important to praise and reward the dog as she stays. This keeps your exchange of qi active with the dog. She needs to know that stay is not a punishment.

Wu Wei: Teaching dogs to stay with rewards while they are performing the task will teach them to stay much more quickly and reliably than will dominance-based methods. Your dog will look forward to sit-stay rather than try to figure out a way out of it. She'll stay firmly in place, waiting for the last available reward for her good behavior. Dogs who are rewarded only at the end of the stay can't wait to end the exercise so they can get their reward.

22

PRACTICAL APPLICATION OF THE TAO:
Teaching Heel

Wild canids follow their pack leaders. If people often laugh at you and your dog and say, "Well, it looks as if your dog is walking you instead of you walking your dog," you are putting your dog in the position of pack leader on your walks.

This makes your walks much less pleasant— and certainly more dangerous—for both you and your dog than if you are in the leadership position when you walk. Because your dog is in the alpha position, he has to be on constant alert on your walks. He is responsible for protecting you and himself from danger. He has to decide if every person, dog, or inanimate object is friend or foe. No wonder he spends so much time sniffing and marking territory. You have essentially told him that is what he is supposed to do by putting him in alpha position. His fight-or-flight response is turned to the full "on" position.

Heeling gives your dog the information that you are the alpha leader in the pack and he needs to follow you. This allows him to relax on his walks. It will decrease his aggression if he is a dominant dog and increase his confidence if he is a shy dog. You will also have the joy of truly sharing together the experience of your walk, which both of you will enjoy.

In formal training, a dog should walk precisely at his human's left side and sit each time the human stops. This formal heeling exercise is handy. I can walk through a crowd of people with one of my trained dogs and know exactly where he is at every moment. I can have my arms full of fresh produce at the local farmers' market and know my dogs will be there safely with me, too close to me to be harmed by another dog or stepped on by a clumsy person.

Although that kind of precision is great, it is unnecessary for most situations. Most people just want a dog who will walk quietly with them on a loose lead. They want the feeling of communication with their dogs, so they can companionably enjoy a neighborhood walk, share the glory of a sunny summer afternoon, and show each other the sights, sounds, and scents of the time they spend together.

I teach my dogs the meanings of two phrases. *Heel* means the formal heel position, where the dog is within a few inches of my side and sits quickly each time I stop. To me and my dogs, *this way* means they walk on a loose leash and just generally pay attention to me.

Both these exercises are taught the same way; the difference is in the expectation you have of where the dog should position himself. All that matters is that you are consistent so the dog can learn the meaning of the word. Thus it is important that *heel* always mean the same thing. If sometimes *heel* means "Walk precisely at my side and sit each time I stop," but sometimes *heel* means "Just keep within a couple of feet of me and don't walk in front where I might trip over you," your poor dog will never understand the exercise.

To start teaching the heel position, let your dog know your left hand is magical. Hold your left hand out to your dog. When he touches it, give him a little treat and lots of praise. Every time he touches your left hand, reward him with generous praise and a treat if one is available. You will be establishing a flow of qi between your dog and your left hand.

Once you have established that flow of qi, walk with your dog. Every time he puts his nose near your left hand, say, "Good heel!" Sometimes give him a treat when he touches your left hand as you walk together. Soon your dog will automatically stay close by your magical left side.

Decide what position you want your dog to place himself into. If walking a couple of feet away is fine, tell him, "Good heel," when he's within your acceptable range, and reward him whenever he is in that range. If you want him to keep himself in a formal heel position, reward him when he has placed himself in that position.

Remember to reward the dog only when he is in the heel position. If you tell him that he is doing a great job and give him a treat when he is leaping about in your face or is pulling at the end of his leash, he will naturally assume that is what he is supposed to do.

Talk with your dog while he is heeling. One of the fastest ways to lose his energy and enthusiasm is to be silent. Keep your pace quick. Make turns, so your dog has to focus on you. Keep the exchange of qi bright and happy.

Those of us who have very small dogs have a special challenge teaching them the meaning of the word *heel*. If my little dogs watch my hand, they will be forced to pull their necks back at an impossible angle when they are in the heel position. This is very bad for their necks and backs and could even lead to an injury. If your dog cannot reach your hand with his nose, teach him to focus on your left leg instead of your left hand. Pick a spot on your left leg at about the level of your dog's nose. Show it to him. When he looks at the spot or touches it, tell him he's a good dog. Give him treats that you hold next to the spot. When you teach him heel, touch that spot on your leg. Give him praise and treats and say, "Good heel," when he walks with you in the correct position with his focus on that spot on your leg. Soon your dog will learn to concentrate on your left leg, just as a larger dog concentrates on his trainer's left hand.

Heeling is fun. Having a reliable heel allows you and your dog to experience great adventures together.

Application of Taoist Principles in Teaching the Word *Heel*

Stillness: Although heel entails more action than any of the other training exercises, your inner stillness is still vital to maintain the link and telepathy between the two of you. Think of your inner quiet as the classic Taoist concept of the stillness within the motion.

The Innate Nature of the Dog: Heeling almost directly mimics dog pack behavior, with the alpha leader deciding the position of the other dogs in the pack. Pack behavior in the wild relates to the excitement and fun of the hunt, so your walks with your dog in a heel position can replicate the camaraderie of your dog's pack-hunting forebears. Heeling should be joyful.

Exchange of Qi: The exchange of qi should be very apparent. The dog should focus on your hand (or leg). You should also be praising the dog, moving quickly, and smiling. Keep a telepathic picture of where you want your dog to position himself.

Wu Wei: The old way of teaching a dog to heel was to yank on his collar whenever he was out of position. By teaching your dog to focus on you and by keeping up a dialogue, you are allowing the flow of qi to teach him the heel position.

23

PRACTICAL APPLICATION OF THE TAO:
Teaching Come

For your dog to be safe in this human world, she needs to come when she is called. She needs to come even when there is a cat she wants to chase. She needs to come even when there is a dog in her territory. She needs to come even when she is at the beach and wants to have fun.

Coming to you should always be a joyful experience. Why should any dog stop chasing a cat (which is a really, really fun thing for a dog to do) to go back to a human who is dour and unexcited and may even punish her? How many times have you seen someone call a dog, then yell at or even hit her for something the dog did before coming to her human? All that dog learned was never to come to the human again.

So calling your dog should be a happy time

for you and your dog. As always, be sure that the word you use to call her is consistent. If you say, "Come," then *come* should always mean "Come clear up to me," not sometimes mean "Just come halfway" or "Just get away from whatever it is you are doing."

Put your dog on a sit-stay, or have someone hold her for you. Go about six feet away, and call her to you. When she comes, love her, feed her, make a huge scene. Let the scene go on and on. Make coming to you the most fun, exciting thing that your dog can possibly imagine.

When your dog is just learning to come to you, don't try calling her when she is staring at a cat or clearly interested in a person across the room. Set your dog up for success, not for failure. Call her off lead only when you know she is absolutely reliable on leash. Over time you can make the exercise more challenging. Make the distances farther, and call her in the middle of distractions. When she comes to you, always make a huge, happy fuss, no matter how much you expect her to come. Remember, the next time you call her, she may have to make the choice of running after a cat (with a car headed her way) or coming to you. Let her know that coming when she is called is always the best thing to do.

What happens if she does not come when you call her in your training session? Get closer to the dog, and let her see the food in your hand. Repeat the word *come.* Start to run away from the dog, so she knows she needs to follow you to get the treat. When she comes to you, love her, praise her, feed her, fuss over her.

Application of Taoist Principles in Teaching the Word *Come*

Stillness: As in the heel exercise, your stillness is within your motion.

The Innate Nature of the Dog: Dogs come to their leaders. Your dog loves you and is an intensely social creature. She wants to come to her loving, gentle leader, who rewards her prey drive with treats.

Exchange of Qi: Your relationship with your dog is proved every time your dog chooses to come to you. It is the pull of your qi and love between the two of you that results in her running to you to be near you.

Wu Wei: Dominance-based obedience teaches come by pulling the dog's leash until she comes to the trainer. Since coming is unpleasant, many dogs come slowly and will not come unless they are on leash. Training through the exchange of qi and love of the dog works far better and more reliably.

24

PRACTICAL APPLICATION OF THE TAO:
Teaching Down

The down position is the most stable position a dog can hold. A dog can remain comfortably in a down for several minutes, so he can be under control for long periods of time. A dog is also far less likely to get up from a down than from a sit, so he is less likely to break away from the exercise and go flying after a stray cat.

The down is the most submissive position in canine behavior. By allowing himself to be in a down position, your dog is signifying that he is accepting your leadership, thus making him very unlikely to chase another creature.

Once a dog understands the meaning of the words *sit* and *stay*, it is usually very easy to teach him to down.

Place the dog in a sit position. Take a treat, and hold it directly in front of the dog's nose.

Bring the treat down in front of his chest; then extend it along the ground between his front legs toward his paws. By this time your dog will eagerly follow a treat anyplace you put it, so he will follow the treat down to the ground and out in front of him. If he does that, he has no alternative but to down. Tell him how good he is and give him the treat. If you have trained your dog in the other exercises outlined in this chapter, he will usually understand and comply with down after he's been shown the exercise just a couple of times.

After your dog thoroughly understands the meaning of the word *down* and will drop quickly to the floor from a sitting position, start teaching him to do random downs. Play with him; then say, "Down," and lure him to the floor. When he drops down, give him the treat and lots of praise. As he learns to do random downs, make your distance farther and farther away when you say, "Down." Eventually you will be able to say, "Down," and your dog will stop whatever he is doing twenty feet away from you and go into an instant down position.

Once your dog understands the meaning of the word *down*, teach him to do a down-stay. Teach the word *stay* just as you did for the sit-stay. Start off right next to your dog, just as you did for the sit-stay. Your dog will have some trouble believing, at first, that you really want him to stay lying down in a submissive posture while you walk away, so it is very important for you to talk with him and reassure him that he's doing a good job. Work with your dog gradually until he is able to do a down-stay for five minutes while you are thirty feet away.

Once you have achieved this level of work with your dog, you have given him the gift of safety. Imagine a dog who sees his human across the street and goes running toward the person he loves. The human sees the car coming down the street, but the dog is too focused on his beloved human to notice. Before the dog gets to the street, the person says to the dog, "Down!"

The dog happily drops to the ground, knowing that down is one of the most enjoyable things he can do with his human companion. The human quickly says, "Stay," and the car passes by without incident. The human runs to his relaxed, safe dog and gives him a huge hug.

Application of Taoist Principles in Teaching the Word *Down*

Stillness: As in the sit, physical stillness will help your dog concentrate. When you are doing random downs and playing with the dog between downs, it is important to keep the inner stillness so your dog keeps connected with you for the upcoming exercise.

The Innate Nature of the Dog: The down, more than any other exercise, is about your relationship with the dog. He will happily lie down and stay in a down position if you are his respected alpha leader. He will fight you every step of the way if you are not.

Exchange of Qi: The trust between person and dog is most evident when the dog is in the vulnerable down position. An exchange of happy, flowing qi is essential for a relaxed, happy down. It is very important for the trainer to visualize the down to reinforce this word with the dog.

Wu Wei: Dominance-based training required a person to place the dog in the down position by force. Think of a 150-pound Mastiff who just does not want to lie down, and you decide which system is easier!

25

PRACTICAL APPLICATION OF THE TAO:
Teaching Stand

When your dog goes to the veterinarian, she will need to be examined throughout her body. If you have just returned after a long hike in the woods with your dog, you need to look over her entire body to ensure she didn't pick up any ticks. To keep your dog's skin and hair healthy, you need to be able to brush her. All these important activities require your dog to be able to stand and allow you or another person to touch her in sensitive places. Help your dog by teaching her the word *stand*.

Place a delicious doggy treat between the fingers of your right hand. Take a couple of steps with your dog in the heel position. Then reach across your body, and gently put your hand with the treat in front of your dog's nose. She will stand still and merrily eat the treat out of your hand, while you keep repeating, "Good stand." She will quickly learn to stand still and wait for the food when you say, "Stand."

Once she understands the word *stand*, teach her to do a stand-stay. Just as you did with the sit-stay and the down-stay, gradually leave the dog and increase the length of the stay and the distance that you can go from her (there is no practical reason for going more than about six feet away from your dog in the stand-stay).

Once your dog does a reliable stand-stay, come back and gently touch her on the back; then give her the treat, and release her. After she's used to that, run your hand down her back. Over time work with your dog so she will do a stand-stay while you thoroughly examine her entire body. After that, grooming and veterinarian visits will be a pleasure and will not be nearly so stressful to your dog.

Application of Taoist Principles in Teaching the Word *Stand*

Stillness: You are asking your dog to stand still without moving her four paws. Your inner calm and still presence are necessary for her to be able to perform this work.

The Innate Nature of the Dog: Your dog will perform this exercise because of her desire to please her leader. You have also molded her prey drive into behavior that causes her to stay still by giving her food rewards for choosing not to move.

Exchange of Qi: While your dog stands patiently as you examine her body, you will feel the intensity of your relationship. The trust and love you feel can occur only in a relationship with a strong exchange of qi.

Wu Wei: Dominance-based obedience requires the trainer to place the dog physically in a standing position and hold her there until the dog understands the concept. You try that with two hundred pounds of Saint Bernard!

SECTION SEVEN

Yin and Yang

26

CREATING A PERFECT BALANCE

The world is made up of opposing forces. The energy from the earth and the energy from the sky. Cool and warm. Female and male. Dark and light. Stillness and movement. Soft and loud.

These opposing forces are called yin and yang in Chinese philosophy. Neither force is inherently good or bad, but too much of one or the other force places a person or an animal out of balance. When yin and yang are in balance, we have the mixture of creative forces that makes us healthy, content, and happy. Your dog needs to have a balance between yin and yang to be healthy and content as well.

Just as it is easy for people in today's fast-paced urban world to lose their balance, so it is easy for our dogs to lose their balance. Like humans, dogs whose yin and yang are out of balance will face physical and emotional problems.

We commonly see very aggressive dogs (who have too much yang energy) and overly submissive dogs (with too much yin energy). Dogs who have phobias or neuroses are showing the outward signs of a creature without the correct balance of yin and yang.

Because we have brought our dogs into our demanding urban world, we have the responsibility to help them achieve the balance that will ensure they are healthy and happy. It is very rewarding when our dogs can share with us in a healthy, long-lived Taoist lifestyle.

27

DOG QIGONG

The ten thousand things carry yin and embrace yang.

They achieve harmony by combining these forces.[8]

Every morning I get up and practice Soaring Crane qigong (pronounced *chee-gong*). Qigong is a form of meditative exercise that uses body position and the intent of the practitioner to bring qi into the body. By directing qi into our bodies, we become healthier and enhance our spiritual practices. My qigong teacher has spent many hours working with me to bring my form into close enough proximity to the classical form to allow the qi to flow into my body.

Many movements of yoga, tai chi, and qigong are based on the movements of animals. In fact, Hua Tuo in ancient times created the movements of five animals into the first forms of meditative, spiritual exercise.

My dogs practice their own form of qigong every day. They didn't need a patient teacher to show them the correct form. Dogs are born as qigong masters. These are the qigong exercises that my dogs practice daily.

Play Bow

When a dog is ready to initiate a rousing game with another dog (or a particularly lucky human), he goes into a play bow. All dogs do it.

Instead of just accepting the play bow as routine dog behavior, look at it for the beautiful form of qigong it is. The dog's forelegs are firmly planted on the ground, absorbing the earth qi. His back legs are straight, with his rump sticking heavenward. His wagging tail mixes the yin qi and the yang qi. He holds the position while he absorbs more and more energy. Suddenly his body is so full of joyful qi that he explodes, jumping into the air and dancing around his animal or human companion. When he tires, he goes back into the play bow, absorbs more qi, and soon explodes again into energetic play.

The next time your dog gives you a play bow, return one to him. Play with him on his own terms. He will delight in the fact that you are sharing the secrets of the Tao with him.

Great Circles of Qi

You've seen your dog get that blissful, glazed look in his eyes. His breathing becomes shallow. He tucks his rear end underneath him and begins to run in wild circles. He runs so fast his movements are a blur. He changes course so abruptly it is hard to believe that some part of him was not left behind. Your dog seems to be overflowing with the joyful life force of his qi and needs to run in great circles just to express his elation. Then, as suddenly as it began, the qigong ends. His eyes get their focus back, his breathing returns to normal, and he rests after the rush of exercise, looking sublimely content.

Fore and Aft Stretching

Yoga, tai chi, and qigong all emphasize gentle stretching to distribute qi throughout the entire body. Dogs do this nearly every time they awaken from naps. Watch as your dog stretches. First he will place his forelegs out in front and stretch his body toward his rear. Then he will put his rear legs behind him and stretch his whole body toward the front. One of my dogs is a particular master of this particular form of qigong. When she stretches, she always grunts contentedly, and I often hear the healthy little popping noises as her energy becomes un-blocked and her qi can move throughout her body.

Relaxation Qigong

When a dog who has been tense decides to re-lax, he shakes all over as if he were flinging wa-ter from his coat. Next time you take your dog to a new place, watch him. He will usually look around and then relax his body just a bit. Then he does his relaxation qigong.

It is a miracle to watch dog relaxation qigong. Your dog will start out shaking his neck so that first the muscles of his muzzle relax, then his face, then his ears, then his neck. The shake goes on down his spine so the muscles of his shoulders shake, then his abdomen, his rear, and finally his tail. As he finishes the shake, he points all four toes. Your dog has just shaken the tension out of every single muscle of his body, and the exercise took only a couple of seconds.

When my dogs do relaxation qigong, I tell them, "Good shake." When we go someplace new, I ask them, "Do you want to shake?" Usually they happily do their relaxation qigong and feel relaxed and comfortable in the new place right away.

Your dog should have the opportunity to do qigong every day. If he has another dog to play with who is of similar size and temperament, that is ideal. If he does not have another dog friend to play with, play with your dog and encourage him to relax. It is vital to his well-being (and certainly won't hurt yours).

28

EXERCISE:
The Magic Elixir

Lao Tzu wrote:

> With things—some go forward, others
>   follow;
> Some are hot, others blow cold;
> Some are firm and strong, others submissive
>   and weak.
> Some rise up while others fall down.[9]

Your dog needs a regular program of exercise that is appropriate for her body type, age, and temperament. The right amount and type of exercise for a two-year-old Border Collie are not appropriate for a twelve-year-old Chihuahua. The correct balancing point of yin and yang is different in these two dogs, and each dog needs the opportunity to have the right amount of exercise to maintain her own healthy balance.

If a dog does not get enough exercise, her qi will express itself in other ways. She will tend to be a problem barker, have separation anxiety, or may be aggressive. She is likely to develop autoimmune diseases.

A less common problem is the dog who is exercised too much for her body type. Many breeds of dogs hugely benefit from the opportunity to go running with their humans, but trying to make a small or short-legged dog develop such an exercise routine is cruel. The dog's life will be shortened by the excessive demands you are placing on her heart, lungs, and joints.

Look at your dog's body type. Is she extremely long-legged and very slender? Then she probably is happiest with the opportunity to run short distances extremely fast. Is she of medium-slender build and automatically goes into a ground-eating trot? This dog needs miles of exercise every day. Is she square and broad-faced? This dog may have to be coaxed into enough exercise to keep her heart and lungs healthy.

Large dogs need large, fenced, safe places to run. Small dogs usually can get their exercise needs met in a small yard or even in an apartment, as long as they have the opportunity to be able to stretch out and really run.

Listen to what your dog has to tell you. If she is bouncing off the walls at night and has trouble concentrating on her training, she needs more exercise. If she droops her head and resists going on a run with you, you are probably pushing her too hard.

If your dog has the right type and amount of exercise, she will be more content and more trainable. If she is aggressive, the right type of exercise will make her more mellow. If she is shy and overly submissive, the exercise will make her more confident. It will bring her yin and yang into balance.

29

PRACTICAL APPLICATION OF THE TAO:
Play with Your Dog

Taoists believe in humor and fun. The happiness of playing with your dog will help you both live longer. Every dog has a favorite game that you can share. For most dogs their favorite game is fetch.

Lessons from the Game of Fetch

Almost all dogs love to fetch. They do it for hours at a time. Over and over again. And over again. And over. And again. Then repeat.

Some demanding fetchers prefer toys with little squeakers in them. When his human stops throwing the toy, the demanding fetcher stands at his human's feet, insistently squeaking and squeaking the toy until the human relents and throws the toy again. It is the squeaking toy that gets the toss! Other dogs are even more insistent in their demands. These dogs throw their toys at their humans' heads until the humans give up and throw the toys yet again.

The next time your demanding animal companion asks you to play fetch with him, do it with gusto. Enjoy the game from the dog's perspective. An athletic dog has a great sense of the qi of his favorite toy. He will sense it hurling through the air behind his shoulder, and pivot heavenward as he snatches the toy in midair. He will joyfully wag his tail at the unexpected bounce of the ball. He will ferret the toy out from behind bushes or underneath the furniture. He will gleefully wriggle his whole body with anticipation, waiting for you to lob the toy into the air so he can leap and catch it before it can hit the ground. He will smile at you when you mix up some "line drives" with the lobs.

While he is playing fetch, your dog is totally in the moment, the goal of all Taoists. He is thinking only about the toy, his relationship with you, and the joy of the game.

What have you given your animal companion by playing fetch with him? The opportunity to balance his yin and yang through healthy, non-violent exercise. Even more important, you have given him the joy of your coming into his world to play his game.

What has your animal companion given you by agreeing to include you in his game? He has invited you into the magical experience of sharing his world.

30

THE YIN AND YANG OF EXPECTATIONS

There is a Chinese legend about a man who complained to his brother about his stupid dog. "The other morning I left the house dressed in white," said the man with the dog. "When I came home that night, I was wearing black. My dog is so stupid that he barked at me because he could not recognize who I was when I wore black." The man's brother, a philosopher, thought about this and then asked, "Tell me, if your dog left in the morning and was white and came back home that night and was solid black in color, would you recognize him?"

We often place expectations on our dogs that we would never apply to ourselves. We expect them to stay home for twelve hours at a time without having the chance to go to the bathroom. We do not place the same expectations on ourselves. We expect to know when to bark and when to be silent—even if those are not the times the dogs' innate nature tells them to act that way. We know that it takes time and patience for someone to teach us new skills, but we are often impatient with our dogs when they need to learn new skills.

When we have a two-way flow of communication with our dogs, we learn what we can reasonably expect from them. A trained dog has a flow of qi with her human that allows her to communicate her needs. She views herself as a working member of her human pack and is proud of her role. The people who live with her are proud of the dog as well. This is a healthy balance of expectations and understanding by both the owner and the dog. This dog has a balance of yin and yang.

In some situations too much is expected of a trained dog. There are some people who take training much too grimly and work their dogs for hours at a time or for days on end without a day off. A dog that has had too much work and not enough play loses her qi. Her head is down; her eyes are dull. A balance between work and play is just as important for a dog as it is for a human.

On the other hand, a dog who is given no expectations by her owner is equally unhappy. She is often almost frantic, trying to communicate. Her qi is misdirected into problem behaviors because she has no bond with her human to focus her qi.

Dogs need a balanced life of expectations. They should not be given impossible tasks, but they should have activities to keep their intelligence and energy focused and alive.

Setting Boundaries

The task of the Taoist dog trainer is to set fair, reasonable boundaries for our dogs without using cruelty to enforce them.

Every dog needs to learn the meaning of the word *no*. It can save her life.

However, there must always be a positive to

balance every negative. When you tell your dog no and she stops the objectionable behavior, praise her. Redirect her energy from the negative activity to a positive one. For example, if your dog is trying to chase a car, tell her no, then redirect her energy into an acceptable activity, perhaps a sit-stay. As the dog sits, praise and reward her for choosing to do the sit-stay.

Never react in anger or use excessive force. That is cruelty and senseless dominance.

If you have more negative than positive reactions to your dog's behavior, your dog cannot trust you and keep an open flow of qi. So to keep a balance, it is essential that every no be followed by your acknowledging the dog when she stops doing a wrong behavior and does a right one.

PRACTICAL APPLICATION OF THE TAO:
Curbing Aggression

Aggression is not normal behavior in dogs. Wolves, African Wild Dogs, and other wild canids have to be able to work cooperatively. Severe aggression is against the innate nature of dogs. When we look at aggression from a Taoist perspective, we find that the aggressive dog has far too much yang energy. To help an aggressive dog, we have to help him collect more yin energy to balance him.

Where does aggression come from?

Irresponsible Breeding. Many breeds have been the unfortunate victims of irresponsible breeding by human beings. I recently read an article by a respected Akita breeder who wrote that two male Akitas should never be allowed to play together because it would inevitably lead to aggression. The people who are breeding those dogs and the thousands like them have created time bombs. Any dog that is unfit to play with another dog just because of his innate nature is not safe to play with young children and cannot be trusted near other animals. If you have a dog who has this inborn problem, you can bring him a long way forward, but you can never entirely trust him.

If you are considering bringing a puppy into your life, watch how he interacts with his littermates. Wrestling and nipping are normal, healthy behaviors, but be very wary if a puppy is biting another one until the other puppy screams. Puppies instinctively bite at your hands; be cautious about one who will not stop biting at your hand after you have clapped your hands loudly and said no. This puppy may be showing aggression rather than normal oral exploration. Most puppies will not raise their hackles or snarl at another dog or human until they are about five months old; be concerned about a puppy who is displaying these behaviors at three months or less. Observe the behavior of the puppy's mother (and father if he is on the premises). Are they friendly and relaxed with other dogs? If they are aggressive, their offspring are highly likely to be aggressive.

Abuse. Many dogs who are abused retaliate by abusing back. These dogs need to learn that not all humans will abuse them. They need to learn to relax and trust.

Putting the Dog in a Situation Beyond His Capacity. Dogs who feel overwhelmed have a fight-or-flight response. This is not just a phrase; they really will run away, or they will bite something. One of the ways to deal with this problem is to develop a relationship that allows the dog's qi to flow directly to you, reducing his fight-or-flight response. As he relaxes and learns the meaning of your words, situations that at one time would have overwhelmed him no longer will do so.

How to Restore Your Aggressive Dog's Yin-Yang Balance

1. *Exercise your dog.* One of the most powerful ways to balance yin and yang is through exercise. Make sure your dog has lots of opportunity to run, even to the point of being tired. Play fetch with him; it's a cooperative, nonaggressive game.

Be careful about the way you play with an aggressive dog, however. Make sure that you do not run with him in a manner that you seem to play the part of prey; otherwise your animal companion may decide to grab you with his teeth and drag you down.

Do not ever play wrestling games with an aggressive dog. He wins that game by physically overpowering you.

Never play tug-of-war with your aggressive dog. It is a game of dominance and can quickly lead to aggression. (Tug-of-war can be a good game to help a very submissive dog with no tendency to bite become more confident; make sure the submissive dog has the chance to win the game sometimes.) The more your dominant dog expresses his energy in healthy, nonaggressive exercise, the less likely he is to express his energy in dominance.

2. *Practice Inner Stillness.* You need to feel your own inner stillness. An aggressive dog is always on edge. When he picks up on your own nerves and fear, he will be placed further on edge. It is of course hard to have a sense of inner calm when you fear the dog may attack something or may even bite you. This will be a good chance to practice your meditative powers. Relax. If you cannot relax, you cannot help the dog.

3. *Be a Gentle Alpha.* Diligently, consistently, and mindfully practice the Taoist alpha routine (page 41). You absolutely must be an aggressive dog's alpha figure. He needs to learn that you are the pack leader and that he

does not need to be. The more he respects your role as leader, the easier it will be for him to let go of his excess aggression.

4. *Teach Attention.* Review the section on teaching attention (page 92). Your dog cannot attack another dog when he is looking adoringly into your face. Help him focus his qi on you, rather than use his energy to fight the rest of the world.

5. *Reward Every Good Behavior.* If your dog does watch me instead of snarls at a passing dog, reward him. If he sits quietly in a situation in which he would have struck out at something in the past, reward him. Make good behavior more fun and more full of attention than aggressive behavior is.

I worked with a family who had a dog who tried to bite every family member and friend when they left the home. The dog was very alpha in the house and did not want anyone he liked to leave him. In addition to working on Taoist alpha, watch me, and training exercises, we began to reward the dog for paying attention when someone left the house. For about a half hour we had different family members and friends go out of the house. As they were leaving, a member of the household held the dog's favorite snack and said, "Watch me." The first time the dog snarled a bit, but he didn't lunge, so we gave him the treat and told him he was good. By about the tenth time a person left the door, the dog ran over to the person with treats and wagged his tail. It was much more rewarding to get a favorite treat than it was to act aggressively toward a departing visitor. The problem was solved.

Think about what causes your dog to behave aggressively and try to create a positive alternative for your dog to enjoy instead.

6. *Deal with Each Problem Early.* Your dog will always give you a warning that he is going to explode. His eyes will focus on the object of his anger. His tail will become erect.

The hair on his back may rise. You can feel his body tense. Deal with the problem at the first signal your dog gives to you. If he is tense walking one direction, turn him around and walk the other way. If he is making eye contact with another dog, get his attention focused on you or get the other dog out of his line of sight.

Even if you have a small dog, it is nearly impossible to stop a fight. If you have a hundred-pound aggressive Rottweiler, you could be killed in the effort. Deal with the problem when you receive your dog's first warning signals, not when it is too late.

7. *Respect Your Dog's Limitations.* Until your dog is thoroughly trained, avoid situations in which he is likely to explode. Creating situations that trigger his aggression will only ingrain his violent behavior.

Your dog may have more space requirements than other dogs. If he is aggressive when a dog comes within three feet of him, be sure no dogs get closer than five feet. If men with beards send your dog into a frenzy, walk away when you see a man with a beard.

Training your dog can provide a permanent cure to much of the problem. In the meantime, provide leadership to him to ensure he will do no harm. Moreover, the less opportunity you give to your dog to be aggressive, the less ingrained the habit will be. Thus the habit will be easier to break.

As your dog becomes well trained, his limitations will gradually recede. If he would lunge at a dog who comes within three feet of him, over time that distance will decrease, and he will eventually be able to be calm when other dogs touch him. However, he can overcome his limitations only with your help through gentle training.

8. *Work Diligently on the Training Exercises.* The more you train the dog, the less on guard he will be and the more he will accept

your leadership. Work especially on the sit-stays and down-stays. These are yin (passive) exercises and will help your dog learn patience and calmness. The more he becomes proficient at his work, the less likely he is to explode in situations that would previously have been completely unmanageable.

32

EATING RIGHT

Taoists believe in long life and healthy food. Your dog should be fed to maximize her health as well. The bodies of our dogs age faster than ours do. Diseases of old age, such as cancer and arthritis, are common in dogs by age ten; they are not common in humans until we reach our sixties. Therefore, it is extraordinarily important that we feed our dogs in ways that will help offset the aging process. That can be hard to do with commercial dog food.

Look at labels. If you do not put artificial colors and preservatives into your own body, don't feed your animal companion these substances. Some dog foods are preserved with substances that are banned for human consumption. For example, ethoxyquin, a preservative used in many dog foods, is a pesticide. There are also industry standards that allow excrement to be included in dog food.

Fortunately there is a rapidly growing market for natural, more healthy pet food. Look for products that are preserved with vitamin E rather than chemical preservatives. Those products will have a freshness date; of course it is important for your dog to consume the food well before the date has expired. New brands of all-natural dog food are coming onto the market at a rapid pace. Many of these new brands do not include animal by-products or animal digest.

Some proudly advertise the manner in which meat is handled at their packaging plants. Look in pet superstores for these healthier brands. Many are also available at dog shows and other major pet events.

It is perfectly all right to supplement your dog's commercial food with small bits of cooked meat, grains, and vegetables. Most dogs love fresh vegetables and do not get that need met in their dog food.

When you give your dog treats for his hard work in training, give her something as healthy as possible. Most dogs love low-fat cheese. You can replace bits of hot dog with bits of baby food hot dogs, which have much less sodium and fat than the ones we adults eat.

Increasing numbers of people are making homemade dog food for their animal companions. This is a wonderful gift for your dog. Make sure, however, you are feeding her a balanced diet for a dog, which is a little different from a balanced diet for a human.

If you insist on your dog's joining you in a vegetarian lifestyle, pay particular attention to the foods she is given. It is difficult, though possible, to give her a dog-healthy vegetarian diet.

Because of the growing demand for information on cooking for pets, over the past few years dozens of books have been published on how to cook for your dog using fresh meats, whole grains, and fresh vegetables. If your local library, bookstore, or pet supply store does not carry any of these books, a good source is the *Dog and Cat Book Catalogue* from Direct Book Service (1–800–776–2665; www.dogandcatbooks.com). This company carries hundreds of dog and cat books. In its most recent catalog at the time of this writing, Direct Book Service carried twenty-six titles on dog and cat nutrition and cookbooks.

Our dogs are given shorter time spans on this earth than we are. We can make those time spans longer and healthier by giving our dogs the best food we can.

33

THE SEASONS OF A DOG'S LIFE

Lao Tzu said, "To die but not to perish is to be eternally present."[10]

In Western thought we usually avoid discussion of illness, aging, and dying. We somehow hope that if we do not talk about death, it will not happen to us or to those we love. But of course we all have only an allotted number of days on this earth. And it is the nature of things that dogs are given fewer days on this earth than their human companions. Taoism provides a reassuring, even positive perspective on the cycle of death and birth.

We all are part of the Tao. All creatures were connected to the Tao before we were in our current physical bodies, and we will be connected to it after we have left these bodies. Our spirits existed as part of the Tao before we took the physical bodies we have in this life; when we die, we free ourselves of our bodily forms and return to the Tao, from which we came. In Taoists texts there are never references to birth and death; there are references only to death and birth. Like the eternal cycle of the seasons, there is nothing sad or wrong with the cycles of our lives.

The exact nature of this rebirth is not made clear in Taoist writings. That is left up to the understanding of the reader. So you may believe that all creatures leave this earthly plane and become part of the joyful, cosmic energy of the universe. You may choose to believe, as Buddhists do, that we are reincarnated into new physical bodies as we learn our life lessons. Under the Buddhist concept of rebirth, your dog may return to live with you in his next lifetime. In fact, in your next lifetime you could return as a dog and your dog might be your human companion.

However you personally envision the next phase of being, Taoist philosophy is clear that our death is no more to be mourned than the beginning of winter or the onset of spring.

In *The Book of Chuang Tzu,* a Taoist master is ill and close to death. He tells his grieving family and friend:

> The cosmos gives me form, brings me to
>   birth, guides me into old age and settles
>   me in death.
> If I think my life good, then I must think
>   my death good.

Finally the master says, "Peacefully we die, calmly we awake."[11]

And so we must face the fact that we will almost certainly outlive our dogs. We have a re-sponsibility to give them a loving and honored transition into their next stage of being. We must respect them in their old age and, when the time comes, help them die peacefully so they may awake calmly.

Practical Application of the Tao: Comforting a Sick or Aged Dog

Your dog becomes frightened when he experiences illness. He will tell you his fears, especially at night. You may hear him pacing. He may pant. He may come to your bed in the middle of the night, asking for help and reassurance.

When your dog is telling you he is afraid, give him comfort. Lie with him in your bed or on the floor. Hold him in your arms. Connect from your heart. Be silent, or talk, or sing, whatever your dog tells you he needs. Sometimes the two of you will need a good cry together. Respect what your dog needs from you. If he needs your calmness, cry when he is not around. If he needs to hear your voice, tell him stories of some of the best times the two of you had together. Do for him what you would want a loved one to do for you.

Do what you can to make him more comfortable. Massage him gently, giving extra attention to his head and back. Feel for muscles that are tense, and gently hold your hands there, helping him relax. Cold temperatures can sap the vital energy from your dog; keep your house warm or make sure your dog has a warm place to nest. Make sure his sleeping place is comfortable for a dog in his physical condition. Give him opportunities for gentle exercise, but do not push him beyond what he chooses to do.

Your emotional and physical support will calm your dog. He will know he is loved and will have the freedom to live in comfort and to pass out of this earthly life with serenity and peace.

Practical Application of the Tao: The Transition from This Life

For some sick and aged dogs, the natural end of their lives will come in their homes. Many people report their dogs coming up to them to say good-bye just before going into their final sleep.

Other dogs will tell you they are ready to die,

and they will ask for your help. If you have a close relationship with your dog, you will know when he is telling you it is time.

For a dog who has been sick and is ready to let go of this life, euthanasia can be a loving release. A painless injection that includes a tranquilizer allows your dog to pass gently into his final earthly sleep. Hold him. Let him feel your love. As his spirit leaves his body, you may feel him say good-bye to you. You may sense that he is joyous, glad to be free of the sick or aged body that has caused him such pain. His life has had its natural course, and he is now free of his physical body and can return to the Tao, from which he came.

Practical Application of the Tao: Dealing with Grief

The Book of Chuang Tzu describes a friend coming over to console Chuang Tzu after the great sage's wife died. The friend was startled to see him pounding a battered tub and singing. When

his friend told Chuang Tzu that his actions were
not right, the master replied:

When she first died, I certainly mourned
just like everyone else! However, I then
thought back to her birth and to the very
roots of her being, before she was born.
Indeed, not just before she was born but
before the time when her body was created.
Not just before her body was created but
before the very origin of her life's breath.
Out of all this, through the wonderful
mystery of change she was given her life's
breath. Her life's breath wrought a
transformation and she had a body. Her
body wrought a transformation and she was
born. Now there is yet another
transformation and she is dead. She is like
the four seasons in the way that spring,
summer, autumn, and winter follow each
other. She is now at peace, lying in her
chamber, but if I were to sob and cry it

would certainly appear that I could not comprehend the ways of destiny. This is why I stopped.[12]

Chuang Tzu mourned his loss for only a certain period of time. There is no dishonor in letting your grief express itself. But then try to let it go. Believe that if this stage of our being can be wondrous, so can the next. Release the spirit of your dog to allow him to go joyfully back to the Tao.

Many humans feel great guilt when our dogs die, even when the dogs lived long and happy lives. We feel as if our dogs were our responsibility, and somehow we have failed when they die. It is not within the ability of humans to dictate the life spans of the creatures of this earth. If you have loved and honored your dog during his lifetime, there is no reason for guilt after his death. Love him in your heart, and go on with your life, accepting new creatures to love.

Practical Application of the Tao: Unexpected Death

Death does not always come peacefully or at the end of a long life. Dogs die when run over by a car or after another type of accident. A medical crisis may develop, and you rush your dog to the veterinarian, only for him to die on the operating table. It is very hard to feel peaceful about your animal companion's death when you did not have the opportunity to say good-bye.

Take the time after your dog's death to say good-bye to his spirit. Wish him well. Grieve. Then begin to go on with your life again. You did not have the power to determine your dog's life span.

Guilt can be especially hard to deal with if your carelessness had some part in your dog's death. If you let your dog off leash and then he darted into traffic, it is easy to feel paralyzed with guilt. At some point you must let go of that guilt. Tell your dog's spirit you love him; tell him you are sorry; tell him you learned the lesson. For you to experience the Tao in your own life, you cannot remain paralyzed with guilt for long periods of time. You must at some point open your heart back to life. Honor your dog's memory by applying the lesson you learned from his death to future experiences.

The loss of our animal companions from this world is an inevitable transition we must face. It is part of our lives, just as the cycle of the seasons is part of our lives. Death and birth are part of those cycles.

The *Tao Te Ching* tells us that to die but not to perish is to be eternally present. Our love and connection with our dogs allow parts of their spirits to be with us every day. Their memory does not perish. Although we will always feel a hole in our hearts where we used to hold our dogs, the love and respect we have for our dogs are eternal.

SECTION EIGHT

The Uncarved Block

34

CRACKS IN THE UNCARVED BLOCK

Nature is perfect. It does not need to be improved upon. The Taoist ideal of the uncarved block reflects the flawlessness of nature. The piece of wood is complete in itself and becomes only less so with the imperfect human hand trying to improve its shape.

Our dogs are perfect just as they are. We cannot improve upon such wonderful creatures. Except, of course, breeders try to. The results can be a tragedy of epic proportions.

The Book of Chuang Tzu warns us:

> One on the true path does not lose his
>   innate given nature.
> To such a man that which is united presents
>   no problem;
> That which is divided is all right;
> What is long is not too long;

That which is short is not too short.

The duck's legs for example are short, but
trying to lengthen them would cause pain.

The legs of a crane are long, but trying to
shorten them would produce grief.

That which nature makes long we should
not cut,

Nor should we stretch what nature makes
short.

That would not solve anything.[13]

Until just over one hundred years ago humans bred dogs to achieve the best working function. These functional breedings basically replicated what nature does. The best herding dogs were bred with the best herders, and the best retrievers were bred with the best retrievers.

Part of the incredible variation among the existing dog breeds came from such functional breeding. Dogs who herded sheep had to be fast, agile, and responsive to their owners' distant verbal and whistled signals. Dogs who hunted vermin had to be courageous and built short and close to the ground. Throughout the world small dogs also flourished and became pampered pets on nearly every continent.

The variations among dogs reflected their functions. Human breeders had essentially performed the work of nature by creating an enormous variety of correct, healthy forms of dogs who were inherently able to perform certain functions. They all were as perfect as the uncarved block.

Then, a century ago, humans created dog shows. The purpose of these shows is not to determine the best hunting dog, vermin catcher, or herder. Rather, the purpose is to select the dog who, according to each breed's standard, *looks* like the dog that does its function best. For the first time in history humans were creating dogs for form rather than function.

Dogs who win at shows tend to have exaggerated traits. Thus, if the breed standard calls for a long coat, the dog with the longest coat usually wins. If the standard calls for a flat face, the flattest face wins. Over time the breed standards were changed to reflect the dogs who were winning in the show ring and became increasingly exaggerated.

Now there are setters with coats that hang nearly to the ground; these dogs could never go out in the underbrush and hunt. There are sheepherding breeds whose fashion is to select the biggest, strongest dog—one who would exhaust herself in just minutes of shepherding work. Selective breeding, often with the best of intentions, has ruined the nature of many noble breeds.

Worse still, the "designer dogs" that such breeding practices have developed are sometimes not capable of living normal, healthy lives. Virtually all Bulldogs must be born by cesarian section, because humans have created a dog with massive shoulders and tiny hips. A large percentage of the puppies of many flat-faced breeds have fatal genetic defects in the development of their palates because of the shapes of their faces. In our desire to have the hugest possible dogs, we have developed animals whose hearts and other organs cannot support the size of their bodies. The average life expectancy for the gentle Irish Wolfhound, the tallest of dog breeds, is *four to seven years*!

What have we done? We have bred so much for form rather than function that our dogs cannot perform the tasks that their innate natures long to do.

Diseases and disabilities run rampant throughout dogs. Eight percent of all Dalmatians are completely deaf by eight weeks of age. Half of all Bedlington Terriers have hereditary copper toxicosis. Weimaraners, along with dozens of other breeds, have constant problems with skin diseases exacerbated by poor immune systems. Potential Poodle buyers are told to make sure the sire and dam have been screened for a page-long list of hereditary blood, skin, bone, and eye diseases.

All these problems were caused by extensive inbreeding and linebreeding, in which close relatives are mated to each other to obtain a uniform, winning show look. Even after all the publicity about these problems, the *American Kennel Club Gazette* still features articles for "master breeders" about how to use a great sire or dam repeatedly on a pedigree to bring about the "perfect" show dog. Even conservative show breeders will tell you, "Limited inbreeding is all right as long as you know what you're doing." But who can know what disease will emerge next year that your inbred dog with its narrow gene pool will be unable to resist?

Fortunately there are some breeders who are working hard to reverse these trends. They are working to improve their breeds by breeding only dogs who have been tested to be free of genetic diseases. Among some breeders there has also been an increased emphasis on participating in performance events in which their dogs actually do the work for which they were bred.

These ethical breeders reflect the philosophy of Taoism. A Taoist "master breeder" would not try to figure out how many times a single show dog can appear on a pedigree. A Taoist master looks to the nature of the dog. The dogs of a Taoist "master breeder" should be bred to have the highest possible likelihood of living long, healthy lives. These dogs should be able to perform the functions that are innate to their natures. Anything less is a gross injustice to the animal companions that every breeder claims to hold close to his heart.

Practical Application of the Tao: Finding a Healthy Dog

There is no guarantee that anyone can make that a dog will have a long and healthy life. However, the best breeders go to great lengths to increase the likelihood the dog will be long-lived and vigorous. Think about the following when considering bringing a dog into your home:

1. *Testing for Genetically Linked Diseases.* Genetically related health problems exist in every dog breed. The best breeders are screening their breeding stock for these illnesses and are spaying or neutering any affected dog. Most breeds should be screened for hip and elbow dysplasia. Breeding stock should be rated "excellent" by the Orthopedic Foundation for Animals (OFA). All breeds should be checked for diseases of the eye and certified free of eye disease by the Canine Eye Registry Foundation (CERF). Other tests are breed-specific. One very readable book that lists health clearances to ask about by breed is *The Perfect Match: A Dog Buyer's Guide* by Chris Walkowicz (Howell Book House, 1996).

2. *Performance Events.* People who care about the innate functions of their dogs give them the opportunity to use their abilities at

performance events. There are herding trials for herding breeds, earth dog events for terriers, hunting competitions for retrievers and pointers, and lure coursing competitions for sight hounds. Breeders whose dogs are successful at these events are still breeding for the dog's ability to perform. One good place to find a breeder is at a performance event for the breed of your choice.

3. *Obedience Competitions.* You may never want to compete in an obedience trial with your dog, but trials are a good measure of a dog's mental and physical soundness. At the advanced levels of competition, dogs must be able to jump, fetch, and find things by scent. If a dog has earned a Companion Dog Excellent (CDX) or Utility Dog (UD) title, her brain and body are very likely to be sound. Look for these titles on a puppy's pedigree.

4. *Checking the Pedigree for Inbreeding and Linebreeding.* Every purebred puppy

should have a pedigree, which is the dog's family tree. Look at it to see how often the names of any of your dog's ancestors are repeated. If you see a breeding pattern on the pedigree that would be illegal in your state if they were humans, do not bring the puppy into your family.

5. *Looking at the Dog Objectively.* If you are looking at dogs in an animal shelter, you will not have the benefit of discussing genetic testing with a breeder. The sweet mixed-breed dog at the humane society may have inherited her mother's ability to hunt and her father's skin allergies. Look at the structure of the dog. Is her face too flat for her to be able to breathe without difficulty? Look for eyelids that have turned into the eyes, which will necessitate surgery. Touch her body all over to see if her back is straight and her legs are strong. Make noises behind her to see if she can hear you. Watch her move to see if she has a strong, effortless gait.

✿   ✿   ✿

Despite everyone's best efforts, it is possible that your dog will develop a physical problem that you will have to deal with. Some of the wisest sages in Taoist stories were physically deformed. Our animal companions with less than perfect bodies certainly deserve our unconditional love. Nevertheless, it is unconscionable for breeders knowingly to create dogs that are highly likely to have significant and often painful health problems just for the sake of an exaggerated breed standard.

Lao Tzu said, "The Sage rejects the extreme, the excessive, and the extravagant."[14] So should every dog breeder.

Mutilation

Some dogs are born with erect ears. Others are born with ears that flop down. That is not good enough for some dog enthusiasts. Ear cropping, which is illegal in Britain and many other nations, is practiced on dozens of breeds in the

United States every day. Puppies have to endure this painful mutilation of their ears just so they can look better in the eyes of certain dog fanciers. Doberman Pinschers with natural ears lose none of their innate nobility. Boxers whose ears flop are just as strong and loyal as those whose ears have been cut. Tiny Miniature Pinschers whose ears are left as nature intended them see themselves as just as big and tough as those whose ears are cut and scarred.

Ears are not the only part of the dog that is cut for no reason. Tails are too. Dogs that have only amputated stumps of tails cannot wag greetings or warn enemies. Is that more beautiful than a dog who can tell us how she feels by wagging qi around with her tail?

If we love our dogs, we should allow their bodies to remain unscarred and unmutilated.

35

Wolf Hybrids

Wolves are perfect, wild creatures. They certainly exemplify the uncarved block.

Dogs are loyal friends of humans and have their own form of perfection.

Only man could decide to mate two perfect creatures and create an imperfect, unhappy creature: the wolf hybrid.

Wolves are wild creatures. They haven't willingly joined humans to become part of our world. Wild creatures cannot find happiness in our homes or yards. It is their nature to be free.

Wolf-dog hybrids are neither wolf nor dog. They are imperfect wolves and imperfect dogs. Do not breed a dog to a wolf or wolf hybrid. Few wolf hybrids ever live out their allotted life spans, because when the wolf instinct comes out (as it inevitably must), the hybrid is too dangerous to live in a human home or yard.

It is a human's ego that would hold a wild creature captive or create a confused mixture of wild creature and tame. It is the domestic dog's way to live with man. It is not the way of the wolf.

36

Too Many Dogs

We love dogs. We treat them as our friends, as our families—except when the kind and sad people who work in animal shelters around the United States every year have to kill millions of dogs who were abandoned by their families.

Unless you are positive that your dog's puppies will have permanent, loving homes, and their puppies will have permanent, loving homes, you should never allow your dog to mate. If your dog has puppies and a puppy's new owner cannot keep the dog, you have a moral responsibility to take the puppy back and give it a loving home (even if the "puppy" is now ten years old). Anything less could be a death sentence that you have personally administered to the puppy.

One of my friends asked me, "If Taoism believes in nature and not altering nature, shouldn't people let their dogs have puppies?" I replied that our dogs do not live in nature. They live with us. There is no predator watching the den to grab puppies when the mother dog goes out to feed herself. There are no famine years when most of the pack dies and the numbers are thinned by nature's way.

Since there is no natural balance, we have two choices. Either we can go on as we are, killing millions of innocent dogs, or we can prevent unwanted pregnancies.

All my friends, including my Taoist friends, limited the number of children they brought into the world. We can do the same for our dogs. It is much more natural to me to spay and neuter my dogs than to know that their puppies or their puppies' puppies will live sad, short lives.

37

THE RESILIENCY OF THE UNCARVED BLOCK

Despite the problems faced by our modern dogs, I hold a Taoist's typical optimistic outlook. Dogs have lived for one hundred millennia with humans, despite the countless horrific things that humans have done to these flawless creatures. Part of the perfect nature of our dogs has been their resilience.

I choose to believe that humankind will decide to stop trying to "improve" dog breeds and just enjoy the intelligent, magical creatures that share our homes. Although show dog "master breeders" continue to inbreed their dogs, the general public is becoming increasingly skeptical of the practice. I believe that the ethical breeders who pay attention to the genetic problems of dogs and breed for working function will gain the respect of people who buy dogs.

The growth of the humane movement with its focus on adopting dogs from shelters and its message of controlling the dog population has certainly been heard by the public.

As we love our dogs, spend time with our dogs, and share the Tao with our dogs, perhaps we humans will become better guardians of these wonderful, magical, perfect creatures.

SECTION NINE

The Equality
of All
Things

38

OUR DOGS AS OUR TEACHERS
AND SPIRITUAL GUIDES

You can teach your dog a great deal. You can help him understand the meaning of dozens, even hundreds of words and phrases. You can give him the skills to be safe and calm in our busy, frightening human world. You can provide him with food and exercise to keep his body healthy and his qi flowing into a graceful old age. Your dog can learn a lot from you.

All teachers know they learn more from their students than the students ever learn from them. And we learn more from our dogs than they learn from us.

Each dog shares his soul with us and teaches us far more than we could ever express in words or even in thought. But because I am a writer, it is my innate nature to need the tangibility of words. So I have written down just a few of the lessons of the Tao that I have learned from dogs I have known and loved.

We All Can Be Healers

Dogs heal the sick just by being there. A dog's qi exudes such unconditional love that he makes us well just by the magic of his presence. If we choose to share the love and warmth of the Tao that we carry, we can become healers like our dogs.

We Can Accept People as They Are

Your dog doesn't care if you gained ten pounds. He loves you just as much when you are unemployed and living in a shack as he does when you are wealthy and living in a mansion. The exterior trappings make no difference to a dog. We can choose to accept our friends—and ourselves—as always being the same no matter what their exterior circumstances may be.

Taoists believe that external trappings are irrelevant. Dogs know this is true.

We Can Live in the Moment

Dogs are masters of the meditative art of living in the moment. When a dog plays fetch, he is not thinking about anything else in the world. When you ask your dog, "Do you want to go for a walk?" he is joyous. At the end of the walk when you ask your dog, "Do you want to go home?" he is equally joyous. Each moment has its own delight.

Life is to be savored as it presents itself to us.

We Can Use Our Senses
to Learn the Truth

When your dog meets a new person, he uses all five senses to learn the truth about that person. He looks at the person's face and at the posture of his body to see if the person is friend or foe. He inhales deeply and learns the person's personal scent and determines if the human is afraid or sick. He listens to the sound of the person's voice to see if the human is friendly. He touches the person with his nose to feel the touch of the human. He will probably lick the person to experience his taste. When our dogs greet a person, they know much more than we do about the character and intention of that human.

Lao Tzu warns us that the sage is guided by what he feels, not by what he sees. If we use our senses in the way our dogs do, we will not be led astray by what we see. With our eyes we can look for the person's body posture instead of just looking at the superficial appearance of his face. We can listen for his tone of voice instead of being distracted by the words he speaks. If we use our own senses of smell and touch, we can pick up fear or anger that we miss when we allow ourselves only to look at the masks we humans put on.

Although dogs learn a great deal by using their five senses, they are not innately suspicious. They are open and honest with strangers. However, they are wise enough to collect information.

We Can Develop Our Sixth Sense

Science has no explanation for most of the abilities our dogs have. Science cannot tell us how a dog wakes up from a nap when his human companion's car turns and heads for home ten miles away. Although dogs have more capacity in their noses, it is not enough to account for the fact that a dog can track a person's footsteps two weeks after he passed by. A flat-nosed Pug with less nasal capacity than any person can be trained to pick out an object that his human companion has touched. Recently two dogs have been trained to sniff for cancer cells. They can find the cells with nearly 100 percent accuracy. No one can tell us how a dog can find cancer in a body that the most sophisticated machines cannot detect.

Taoists have an explanation for our dogs' extraordinary capacities. When we are in the Tao, our senses are heightened. We can see and hear things we could not when we put all our energy

on superficial human creations. Dogs live the
power of the Tao every day.

We Can Connect with
Each Other Every Day

Dogs connect with their loved ones every day.
When you come home from work, your dog
gives you his greeting: a happy wiggle and a
touch of the nose. When strange dogs meet, they
have a stylized greeting to determine their place
in the hierarchy without violence. When dogs
play together, they start with a touch of the nose
and a play bow.

Dogs teach each other how to greet and play.
Watch a dog who has been socially sequestered
throughout his life in a kennel or other isolated
environment. He does not know how to greet
other dogs. If he is exposed to other dogs, they
will show him what to do. Once I had the moving experience of watching a happy, well-adjusted dog teach a dog who had spent her life in
a cage how to do a play bow.

Your dog can teach you to be connected with everyday life just the way the well-adjusted dog taught the kennel dog. Watch how he takes the time to greet you and reconnect his qi with yours every time he sees you. Do the same for him and for the humans in your life. You all will be more connected and loving. Watch how he tells strangers that he is no threat. Do the same with a smile and a greeting. You'll find that strangers will treat you more kindly. Your dog invites his friends to play with a play bow. You can invite your friends to play too.

The quality of our relationships with one another is determined by the flow of qi we allow to pass between us. Dogs know the importance of contact in helping the qi to flow.

We Can Learn Humility

Your dog doesn't think he is someone important. He doesn't require people to address him with titles. He just goes about his life, wagging his tail, and enjoying the moment.

He doesn't ask flocks of people to come to him. But they do. Try to walk down a busy sidewalk with your dog without being stopped a dozen times by people who just want to touch him. In his humble way your animal companion undoubtedly affects the lives of those people more profoundly than any activity you have carried out on your job that day.

By being humble and happy within himself, your dog is infinitely powerful. We too are more powerful when we cast off our affection for our titles and social positions and choose to be happy being the persons we are.

We Can Enjoy the Gift

It is a constant wonder that this creature came to join humankind at the dawn of our history. Each day at our side we have an extraordinary friend. He is loyal, loving, and kind to us. He is our companion even when we are sick and sad—especially when we are sick and sad. He protects our homes for us. He plays with us and takes us with him on his walks. He listens to our secrets and knows they are important to us.

Our dogs are a bridge between the awesome life forces of the universe and the world that humankind has built for themselves. They bring us back to our sense of nature. They bring home to our sense of magic. They show us how to find the Tao within ourselves.

Then they wag their tails.

Works Cited

1. Gia-Fu Feng and Jane English, *Lao Tsu: Tao Te Ching* (New York: Vintage Books, 1972), ch. 1.
2. Martin Palmer with Elizabeth Breuilly, *The Book of Chuang Tzu* (London: Arkana, 1996), p. 72.
3. Robert G. Henricks, *Lao-Tzu: Te-Tao Ching* (New York: Ballantine Books, 1989), p. 74.
4. Palmer and Breuilly, op. cit., pp. 32–33.
5. Henricks, op. cit., p. 89.
6. Feng and English, op. cit., ch. 78.
7. Ibid., ch. 64.
8. Ibid., ch. 42.
9. Henricks, op. cit., p. 81.
10. Feng and English, op. cit., ch. 33.
11. Palmer and Breuilly, op. cit., p. 54.
12. Ibid., p. 151.
13. Ibid., p. 67.
14. Henricks, op. cit., p. 81.